Praise for
Moxie
and John Baldoni

"John Baldoni is a prolific thought leader. With *Moxie*, he helps leaders recognize the fire that drives them. Touching on leadership, innovation, and engagement, John brings to life the excitement that drives us all to strive for the pinnacle of success which is often quite elusive. *Moxie* is a must-read for any C-level manager or executive who wants to bring the energy back to their life and their career."

—Marshall Goldsmith, Top 50 Thinker and
best-selling author of *What Got You Here
Won't Get You There* and *MOJO*

"John Baldoni's newest offer *Moxie,* is a valuable book for today's leaders. Drawing on examples from great trailblazers of the past, Baldoni shows how effective leaders work and behave with passion and purpose. Brilliantly integrating the traditional psychology of self-awareness with the critical need for people skills and resiliency, *Moxie* proves to be the whole package. Highly readable and inspiring!"

—Stephen M. R. Covey, best-selling author of
The Speed of Trust and co-author of *Smart Trust*

"Mindfulness, Opportunity, X Factor, Innovation, Engagement. MOXIE. Just what corporate America is missing today. John Baldoni is known for coaching high-level executives as well as for his columns and books. Whether starting out with an innovative idea that is attracting investors or well established and sitting in the corner office, John's new book should be on the must-read list for those striving for excellence and success."

—Mike Myatt, best-selling author of *Hacking Leadership*
and *Forbes* leadership columnist

"With *Moxie*, John Baldoni explores what it takes to lead from the inside out. By focusing on mindfulness, Baldoni demonstrates how leaders can use their inner resolve to paint a picture of the future and overcome obstacles in order to achieve success for the organization."

—Gary P. Von Kennel, retired global CEO of Rapp Worldwide and former CEO of Tracy Locke Advertising

"*Moxie* is that rare leadership book that is both fresh and enduring and will make you think about how you lead. A coach at heart, John has written a must-read for aspiring leaders as well as CEOs in a style that resembles a great conversation with a good friend. Bookstores are filled with leadership books that try to capture the next big leadership thing; in *Moxie*, John offers the big things that endure and help leaders succeed regardless of industry or environment. If you are a leader, this book will serve as a trusted resource for years to come."

—Brian Layer, CEO of N2growth and retired brigadier general in the U.S. Army

MOXIE

MOXIE

THE SECRET
TO BOLD *and* GUTSY
LEADERSHIP

JOHN BALDONI

First published by Bibliomotion, Inc.
39 Harvard Street
Brookline, MA 02445
Tel: 617-934-2427
www.bibliomotion.com

Library of Congress Cataloging-in-Publication Data

Baldoni, John.
    Moxie : the secret to bold and gutsy leadership / John Baldoni.
        pages cm
    Summary: "In Moxie: The Secret to Bold and Gutsy Leadership, author John Baldoni uses concrete, tried-and-true steps to bring out the inner leader in everyone. For management and employees alike, Moxie provides a roadmap to inspire innovation and effective leadership"— Provided by publisher.
    ISBN 978-1-62956-021-2 (hardback) — ISBN 978-1-62956-022-9 (ebook) — ISBN 978-1-62956-023-6 (enhanced ebook)
    1. Leadership. 2. Courage. I. Title.
    HD57.7.B34897 2014
    658.4'092—dc23
                                                                    2014017406

For my daughter Ann Baldoni
who knows what moxie is because she lives it

Also by John Baldoni

The Leader's Guide to Speaking with Presence: How to Project Confidence, Conviction and Authority (2013)

The Leader's Pocket Guide: Indispensable Tools, Tips and Techniques for Any Situation (2012)

Lead with Purpose: Giving Your Organization a Reason to Believe in Itself (2011)

AMA Handbook of Leadership, edited by Marshall Goldsmith, John Baldoni, and Sarah McArthur (2010)

12 Steps to Power Presence: How to Exert Your Authority to Lead (2010)

Lead Your Boss: The Subtle Art of Managing Up (2009)

Lead by Example: 50 Ways Great Leaders Inspire Results (2008)

How Great Leaders Get Great Results (2006)

Great Motivation Secrets of Great Leaders (2005)

Great Communication Secrets of Great Leaders (2003)

180 Ways to Walk the Motivation Talk, coauthored with Eric Harvey (2002)

Personal Leadership: Taking Control of Your Work Life (2001)

180 Ways to Walk the Leadership Talk (2000)

Contents

Acknowledgments

Moxie represents many of the ideals I have observed in men and women in leadership positions. The influence of these remarkable people has enabled me to develop a book that will help others achieve their own leadership potential.

I owe special thanks to the leaders who shared their time with me during interviews and research sessions. They are Fernando Aguire, General John Allen, Donald Altman, Doug Conant, Chester Elton, Mark Goulston, Adam Grant, Jim Haudan, Jim Kouzes, Ryan Lance, and Richard Sheridan. Their insights have made for a better book, and I am grateful to each of them.

I want to single out Rich Wellins, PhD, of DDI for allowing me to cite DDI's excellent research. The same applies to the Hay Group for allowing me to cite their global studies on leadership.

I want to thank my agent, Eric Nelson of Susan Rabiner Literary Agency, for believing in this book, as well as in me. Eric provided me with insights that helped me sharpen the focus of the book. Sarah McArthur was my personal copyeditor, and to her I am grateful. Jill Schoenhaut masterminded production, and Susan Lauzau worked her magic with the copy.

Mike Myatt, my colleague at N2growth, has been supportive in this project, and I want to say a special thank you. Tyler Walker, the Creative Director at N2growth, designed the infographics for which I am very appreciative. (Ty's giving up his art for medical school. A loss for me but a boon to mankind.) And lastly, I want to thank my wife, Gail Campanella, for her faith in me and my work. Thanks again, sweetheart.

List of Experts

The following people were interviewed for their insights into how leaders apply the principles of Moxie to bring people together for common purpose.

Fernando Aguirre, former CEO of Chiquita Brands

General John Allen, U.S. Marines (retired), commander of NATO forces in Afghanistan (2009–2011) and special deputy for the Middle East for Secretary of State John Kerry

Donald Altman, MA, LPC, psychotherapist and author of *One-Minute Mindfulness* and *The Mindfulness Code*

Doug Conant, former CEO of Campbell Soup Company and coauthor of *TouchPoints*

Chester Elton, "The Apostle of Appreciation," coauthor of *The Carrot Principle, The Orange Revolution,* and coauthor with Adrian Gostick of *All In: How the Best Managers Create a Culture of Belief and Drive Big Results*

Mark Goulston, MD, executive coach, founder of Heartfelt Leadership, and author of *Just Listen* and *Get Out of Your Own Way at Work*

Adam Grant, PhD, professor of management at the University of Pennsylvania Wharton School, and author of *Give and Take*

Jim Haudan, CEO of Root, Inc., and author of *The Art of Engagement*

Jim Kouzes, Dean's Executive Fellow of Leadership, Leavey School of Business, at Santa Clara University and coauthor with Barry Posner of more than thirty leadership books and workbooks, including *The Leadership Challenge*

Ryan Lance, CEO of ConocoPhillips

Richard Sheridan, cofounder and CEO of Menlo Innovations and author of *Joy, Inc.: How We Built a Workplace People Love*

Prologue

Give me a place to stand, and a lever long enough, and I will move the world.

ARCHIMEDES

Moxie!

The very word conjures up images of tough-talking guys with bent noses and fedoras pulled down low over their eyes. It is a word that was common in the 1930s and typically associated with people born on the wrong side of the tracks. Common people to whom circumstances had not been kind. They had to make do with what they had, even if it meant using their fists. Prizefighters were said to have moxie, an inner sense of toughness. They knew how to fight as well as how to take a punch. They were tough guys, and the hard knocks they had endured showed on their faces.

Three-quarters of a century later, moxie is not a commonly used word, but it is one that is a favorite of mine. I like to apply it to leaders who have an inner sense of toughness. Most do not come from a hardscrabble or mean-streets background, but all have endured a number of fights, not in the ring nor in places they had to use their fists, but they were punchers all the same. They're guys and gals who had what it takes to lead others in tough circumstances.

Moxie is the essence of what makes a leader tough on the

inside and soft on the outside. These people know what it means to get knocked down, but better still, they know how to get back up. They also stick up for others, especially when the chips are down, and you want them on your side. And lucky for you, they most often are.

By definition, moxie is gumption (*get up and go*), guts (*courage*), and determination (*perseverance*) all rolled into one. These are traits any leader needs, but to me there is another aspect: Moxie was the name of a soda pop, a carbonated soft drink. And so, without stretching too much, you can put a little sugar on the concept, because tough leaders have appeal, a little honey that draws people to them. They are likable.

Why Moxie?

After the financial crash of 2008, we often heard senior executives declare that they'd never seen things so bad. Trust in management plummeted. A survey of senior leaders conducted by Booz Allen in early 2009 showed that 46 percent of those surveyed doubted their CEOs had a credible plan to deal with the crisis, and 50 percent doubted that their company had the leadership necessary to execute such a plan. This lack of confidence did not come from rank-and-file employees, but rather from the senior-most leaders of organizations. That's pretty damning.

As with most crises, it passed, but its wake left devastation in terms of loss of wealth, jobs, and, frankly, confidence in leaders. Slowly but surely wealth and jobs have been restored—not as much as we've hoped—but the trends are positive. Except for those regarding leadership. According to the National Leadership Index for 2012, compiled by the Center for Leadership at Harvard Kennedy School, 69 percent of Americans surveyed viewed leadership in crisis mode. Not unexpectedly, faith in government and corporate officials has eroded over time. But there is hope, because when respondents were asked how America could solve its problems, 81 percent said, "effective leadership."

Leadership post-crash is not really any different from leadership pre-crash, except for one thing: resilience. Those who have steered their companies back to prosperity did it by making tougher, wiser choices and moving forward in hard times. In short, these leaders have "moxie."

Flash-forward to the present. In my coaching, I have the privilege of working with men and women at every level in organizations, but as my practice has evolved I've begun to focus on those at the top of their game, those who are leading their organizations. They have guts, gumption, and they know how to get glory—for their teams, their companies, and, yes, themselves.

These folks have moxie, and it's something that every leader would do well to put into practice. I define it as one part courage, one part can-do spirit, and one part recognition. In *Moxie*, I explore how the concept focuses on what leaders need to be as well as what they need to do. In short, moxie is an acronym...

Specifically, leaders need to be mindful of their circumstances as well as of their strengths and shortcomings.

Leaders must be opportunistic in the sense that they want to make positive things happen. They also need to have the disposition to succeed as well as the inner resourcefulness to persevere. Leaders know that risk is involved with most ventures, so they must be willing to do things differently. They must be innovators.

And all good leaders know that they, by themselves, accomplish very little. They must engage with others in order to achieve sustainable goals for themselves, their teams, and their organizations.

Moxie is an attribute that successful leaders use to make a positive difference in the world in which they live.

Leaders with moxie have four key attributes:

Fire. Leaders with moxie burn with a desire to make something happen. They have a passion for what they do, whether it's building a business or running a small nonprofit. They have a need to make a positive difference in the lives of others.

Drive. Leaders with moxie have ambition. They want to get ahead, and for that reason they will make short-term sacrifices for long-term gains. Their ambition is not all personal. They want others to share in their own good fortune.

Resilience. Leaders with moxie know how to pick themselves up after a fall. They have known defeat, and it does not scare them. It only provides the motivation to get back up and try again, not necessarily the same way.

Street smarts. Leaders with moxie know how the world works. They know how to read people, those who are with them as well as those who may be against them. They have a good sense of what makes people tick and for that reason they are pretty savvy when it comes to making deals.

Speaking realistically, leaders with moxie are those who have the:

- *Competence* to do their jobs—they are often called "go-to people."
- *Credibility* to bring people together—people trust them to do the right job at the right time with the right resources.
- *Confidence* to believe in themselves as well as in the strengths of others—in short, people feel better being around them.

Put these characteristics together and you have a person who knows himself and what it takes to get ahead. A leader with moxie wants to be in charge. He loves the responsibility that comes with setting the course for others to follow. He is accountable.

A leader with moxie is dependable. She can be counted on to do the right thing and to bring others together for common purpose. She is a straight shooter, and for that reason people like being around her.

We can also look at moxie as a means of dealing with the world at large. Consider moxie as an acronym.

Mindfulness. People with moxie know that good things happen to people who seek them. Such folks are aware of their situation and, most importantly, are aware of their ability to effect positive change.

Definition: A mindful leader knows the situation as well as his capabilities and those of the people around him.

Opportunity. Individuals with moxie do not wait for things to come to them. They look for new opportunities. They are seekers of the new and different.

Definition: An opportunistic leader looks for ways to make things better. She is motivated by a desire to make a positive difference.

X factor. Each of us has a unique set of talents and skills that we use to make our way in the world. More than talent, it is what makes you, you—your character, convictions, and personal beliefs. Consider this set the X factor: what enables you to do what you do and do it well.

Definition: A leader with the X factor has what we call "the right stuff of leadership." She radiates character and uses her ambition to focus on the right goals. She has the persevering spirit that radiates resolve. Leaders with the X factor are humble, and their humility attracts others to them.

Innovation. Individuals who have moxie are not content with the status quo. They continually seek to acquire new skills and apply them in new ways.

Definition: An innovative leader knows that life is not lived in a linear fashion. Sometimes you need to take risks. That means thinking differently, doing differently, and rewarding others who do the same.

Engagement. People with moxie seek to engage with the wider community. They are focused on making a positive difference in their teams and in their organizations.

Definition: An engaged leader knows that he can achieve little by himself. These leaders engage the talents, but more importantly, the enthusiasm and spirit of others in order to achieve results that enrich, reward, and perpetuate the organization.

Throughout this book you will read interviews with CEOs and thought leaders whose experience in leadership positions gives them the authority to illustrate the attributes of moxie based on their own experience. These interviews, coupled with the stories of the men and women profiled at the head of every chapter, present a portrait of moxie that reveals character, courage, determination, and resilience that are instructive as well as inspiring. My approach in *Moxie* is to show rather than tell. That is, I want the leaders whom I have selected to present their ideas and insights in ways that will engage your mind, stimulate your innovative spirit, and provide a foundation for continued leadership growth.

Those leaders who put moxie into practice are those who prepare themselves for the constancy of change and set an example for others to follow. Moxie then becomes a principle by which individuals can put their leadership selves into gear in order to accomplish a goal for themselves, their teams, and their organizations. In *Moxie*, we will see how individuals with moxie at their core succeed.

Leaders with moxie are those to whom others look for guidance as well as inspiration.

Moxie lives!

$$\text{Moxie} = \frac{\textbf{Guts + Gumption + Determination}}{\textbf{Goals}}$$

1

Mindfulness

From the quiet reflection will come even more effective action.

PETER DRUCKER

Wisdom of Perhaps

Donald Altman, psychotherapist and author of books on mindfulness, likes to tell a story that he calls "The Wisdom of Perhaps." The tale has been told and retold in many different forms, but here's a quick synopsis.

A man comes home early from work and his neighbor asks him why. The man replies that he has just lost his job. The neighbor says, "That's the worst thing that could happen to you." The man replies, "Perhaps."

A day or so later the man encounters an old friend in the banking industry. When the friend learns that the man is out of work, he offers him a job as a senior executive right on the spot. The man accepts and the next day arrives at work so early that the moving crew is still there. The man lends a hand and, as luck would have it, wrenches his back and goes home. When the neighbor hears what happens, he says, "You're the unluckiest guy in the world." To which the man replies, "Perhaps."

The next day the bank is robbed and employees are held hostage, and of course the neighbor has a response. "Boy, are you lucky you hurt your back." "Perhaps," the man replies.

Events occur, often outside our control. What we can control is our response to those events. As Altman explains, "One little event doesn't define us, one adversity doesn't define us." Often when we reflect on our lives, according to Altman, "Adversity actually has a silver lining. So we can take the attitude of *perhaps* with us on a daily basis."

Mindfulness gives individuals the perspective to take a step back and reflect on the situation. Things can be bad, of course, but it falls to the leader to seek to make things better.

Mindfulness. People with moxie know that good things happen to those who seek them. Such folks are aware of their situation and, most importantly, are aware of their ability to effect positive change.

Nelson Mandela

Nelson Mandela liked tea.

Certainly he enjoyed the briskness of an afternoon cup. Or perhaps he liked the fact that it was a habit of the English, one he had learned while studying law at Oxford as a young man. Whatever his reasons, Mandela used the ritual of afternoon tea

OF TOP 20 COMPANIES FOR LEADERSHIP, RESPONDENTS SAY THAT:

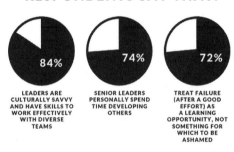

84%
LEADERS ARE
CULTURALLY SAVVY
AND HAVE SKILLS TO
WORK EFFECTIVELY
WITH DIVERSE
TEAMS

74%
SENIOR LEADERS
PERSONALLY SPEND
TIME DEVELOPING
OTHERS

72%
TREAT FAILURE
(AFTER A GOOD
EFFORT) AS
A LEARNING
OPPORTUNITY, NOT
SOMETHING FOR
WHICH TO BE
ASHAMED

SOURCE: 2013 BEST COMPANIES FOR LEADERSHIP HAY GROUP[1]

as an extension of his warm and open personality, particularly when greeting guests. Tea, which he always insisted that he pour, also became a symbol of control.

When, after nearly decades of captivity, it became apparent that he would eventually be released, the South African government decided that it must learn to deal with Mandela as a political force that might one day rule the country. For that reason, the prison authorities gave him his own house on the grounds of a mainland prison, and when government officials came calling, Mandela played host. Even though he was a prisoner, he was the master of his house. He was its lord as well as the designated tea pourer. In this way, Mandela slowly, and not coyly, asserted himself as one who must be reckoned with.

World leaders come and go, but few have captured the imagination like Nelson Mandela. Born into royalty in his homeland, he assumed chiefly duties. Seeking wider influence, he soon ran smack into the vicious and oppressive apartheid system designed to keep black Africans, the overwhelming majority, in a state of subjugation.

As head of the African National Congress, Mandela was tried on terrorism charges and sentenced to five years in prison in 1961. He was sent to Robben Island, a remote spit of rock in the Indian Ocean, four miles off the coast of Cape Town. Later, when his papers were found in a distant farmhouse, Mandela, still in prison, was tried on treason charges and sentenced to death. His death sentence was later commuted but the hardships endured. He pounded rocks in the blazing sun day after day, years upon end. It was mindfulness, as well as the cohesion of his comrades on Robben Island, that enabled him and his fellow prisoners to persevere.

While such treatment may have broken a lesser man, it only fueled Mandela's conviction. On the plus side, he was surrounded by his brothers in arms, fellow members of the ANC. In time, he was hailed as the hero of the liberation movement in South Africa, which gained momentum during the years of his incarceration.

During this time, Mandela looked forward, and in doing so, learned Afrikaans, the language of his jailers, as well as Afrikaner culture. He came to understand that, unlike the English, who might re-emigrate to Britain or another commonwealth nation like Canada or Australia should black people come to government, the Afrikaners, descendants of Dutch farmers who had emigrated to Southern Africa in the seventeenth century, were home. They referred to themselves as Africa's White Tribe, and they were not going anywhere.

After Mandela was released to worldwide acclaim and

adulation in 1993, he traveled the world. When it was decided that there would be free and fair elections, he ran for president and won. This thrilled the hearts of his fellow Africans, but absolutely terrified the whites. Mandela, being a wise man with a capacity for human understanding that dwarfed most others, understood that he needed to pull the nation together. His method was rugby. South Africa, long banned from international sports competition, was designated the host nation for the Rugby World Cup of 1995. This was a huge deal for the Afrikaner population, less so for fellow Africans. But Mandela understood that this was his opportunity to make a statement to Afrikaners that he needed them as partners in the government as well as partners in the nation.

As told in the book *Playing the Enemy* (and later depicted in the movie *Invictus*) Mandela ensured that Afrikaner tradition in rugby would be upheld. The Springbok emblem, a symbol of oppression to Africans, was allowed to remain as the symbol of the team. The team itself was all white save for one player of mixed-race background. Mandela took personal interest in the team, in particular its captain, Francois Pienaar, and in doing so he helped infuse the team with a sense of playing for their country—white and black. The Springboks were underdogs, but with a sense of destiny pulled off the upset of the era, ensuring that, if only for a moment, there was one South Africa.

Only someone with Mandela's sense of purpose could have shepherded a nation whose government was so virulently racist through a peaceful transition that facilitated reconciliation and allowed the country to survive.

Myth surrounds Mandela, and on the one hand it's glorious and fitting. Few men have ever endured such oppression and emerged so unscathed, at least in a moral sense. He was kind, compassionate, and generous, but he was also steeled for his duty. He suffered losses in his family, and eventually in his marriages, but he remained true to his cause.[2]

*****

Mandela exemplifies what it means to be mindful: aware of your situation but at the same time focused on what you can do to improve it. Many people saw the need for change in South Africa, but only a few activists were willing to take the risks involved to fight this uphill battle. Luckily, for most of us the stakes are not so high; still, we can all learn from Mandela's example and it holds relevance for us today.

One of the things I like to do when I begin a coaching engagement is ask my new client this question: What gets you up in the morning? If I see a smile come to the person's eyes, I know that I have tapped into something powerful—what he enjoys doing. The answers are as varied as the executives. Some get excited by tackling new challenges; others enjoy problem solving; others like the thrill of competition; and many like working with their teams to achieve intended results. The answers to this question open the door to greater understanding. When an executive says he likes to see what his team is accomplishing, I know that I am working with an individual who is placing an emphasis on the right thing, working with the team. On the other hand, if the individual says she likes working on projects and contributing in that way I realize that she is more suited to being an individual contributor.

The most troubling answer, or, more precisely, nonanswer, comes from the individual who shows little interest in the work. His answer may be a symptom of burnout or it may be an indication that he does not find the work challenging. In either case, this person is going through the motions. It happens to the best of us. Situations at work may change, so what we once liked to do is no longer possible or we lack the motivation to continue much longer.

My advice is to find something else about the job that you love. Or perhaps look to things you like to do outside of work. Tap into your passion. When the low point comes, and most worthwhile endeavors have a moment when the obstacles look large, you will need that passion to push you through it.

Self-Awareness

Knowing what gets you enthused comes down to self-awareness. The capacity to know oneself is essential to being a leader. Self-awareness is the ability to understand yourself as well as to know how others perceive you. Too often, we overlook self-awareness as an important attribute of strong leadership.

According to a 2012 survey of 17,000 employees, conducted by the Hay Group, only 19 percent of executives possessed a degree of self-awareness. As Ruth Malloy, a vice president with Hay Group, put it in an interview: "If you think about most people in our day-to-day lives, we tend to run on autopilot. We often are not mindful about our impact on others or how and when we spend our time. We can easily get caught up in the task or the day-to-day distractions."[3] As a result we lose touch with ourselves. How we build our self-awareness says something about how we will succeed as leaders. The first step is acknowledging that we have work to do. Often that comes from feedback we receive from a trusted source, be it a boss or a colleague. Applying that feedback so we make positive changes is essential. Malloy told me, "Developing self-awareness requires reflection." This echoes advice I have heard from other executives that you, as a leader, must build reflection time into your schedule. It could be alone time; it could be time shared with colleagues. The point is to find an opportunity to get perspective on your situation and think about what you need to do next. Or, as Malloy said, to think about "how you could react differently in the future."[4]

It is not unusual, for example, for a leader to have a number of employees who liked the old way the company did things, and who find her passion frightening. If you are not aware of what others think of you or the situation, then it can be difficult to connect with them. Leadership requires persuasion, and that can only occur if the parties understand each other. We develop self-awareness when we take time to learn from others as well as listen to what others tell us. Self-aware leaders know what is happening around them; they live in the present but are aware of the future. They know that what they do has consequences, and for that reason they are attentive to how they interact with others.

The fact that so many executives are lacking in self-awareness resonates with my work in coaching.[5] I like to say that executives are so busy focusing on others that they often overlook themselves, specifically the effect their actions may have on others. This is not always bad. An executive who is setting the right example in terms of his communications may not be aware of how well he is connecting with others. By contrast, a manager who is deficient in his ability to delegate work may not realize how much of a micromanager he has become. Self-awareness is fueled by mindfulness, the ability to think and act in the present. Mindfulness is a state of being, and it requires attentiveness to the here and now as well as to what is happening with others.

Self-Knowledge

Savvy leaders develop self-knowledge through mindful practice. It can begin with patience. For the many leaders whose internal motor powers them to act, the concept of patience can seem foreign. It can be perceived as passivity. In actuality, patience is an active process. While we cannot control the situation, we can control how we react to it.

Mindfulness, as described by psychotherapist and best-selling author Donald Altman, enables us "to find a state of equanimity." As Altman says, "The brain is Velcro for negativity, and so we can be tilted emotionally in a way that does not allow us to be effective."[6] Mindfulness enables us to check our emotions so we can discern things with a clearer perspective. As such, mindfulness enables us to listen, engage, and connect with others in a more open and honest way.

"The interesting thing is that mindfulness changes our experience of whatever is happening," says Altman. We may harbor negative thoughts or feelings, but when we apply mindfulness we change the experience. We put it into perspective and, therefore, as Altman says, we can observe it. "The emotion becomes the object of our attention," not the subject of it. This distancing enables us to separate the negative thoughts from individuals and in doing so remain more focused and more attentive. "What we're doing is we're calming ourselves and we're observing in a neutral, nonjudging way," Altman says. "It's a major shift in perspective."

"Mindfulness lets you see things in a very fresh way," says Altman. "Think about when you were a child and you had that childlike ability, that first time that maybe you saw that flower or the first time that you witnessed something in nature and were just so engrossed in it, right? And so I think what happens with mindfulness, we start to see things in a very fresh and childlike way. I like to say there's déjà vu, having been there before, mindfulness is more like *vuja de*, never having been there before."

For example, you go into a supermarket and every cashier point is five deep with customers, each pushing a large basket. You move to the self-checkout line and the lines are just as long. You can't control the crowd, but you can control your response. To be honest, when I see lines like that I am tempted to exit and shop someplace else, but in reality that would probably end up costing me more time. So I have learned, with much effort, to fall into the line and wait. My trick is to smile, even though inside I am roiling with irritation. I will chat with fellow customers, and when I get to the cashier, finally, I will not say something nasty—though I may be tempted—I will make light of the situation and talk about how much I enjoyed standing in line.

Silly, yes, but I am the one maintaining composure. I am exerting my patience so that I do not do something stupid and yell at the cashier, who is not at fault for the long lines. It does no good to yell at the manager either. Suggesting that he implement a better time- and work-flow management system makes you sound like a jerk.

Patience, as our mothers taught us, is a virtue. When it comes to mindfulness, patience is the door opener that makes time for us to notice things around us. Applying patience in the workplace means making time for employees and keeping an open-door policy so employees feel free to come in and chat. It sends a signal that you value their contributions.

Mindfulness also means you make time to reflect on what you observe and what you hear. It does no good to listen and not act. That is, when you hear about things going wrong, as a manager you need to find a solution, or better yet delegate someone to get the resources to solve the problem for the team.

Mindfulness requires practice. Consider it, says Altman, "as an awareness of the body...and the mind." The process is "experiential." You build up the practice of it through disciplined observation and being present but also through physical action. Breath control is key. By focusing on breath, something borrowed from yoga, the individual can slow down the external world and focus on the internal.

"Mindfulness is a practice; it's a skill, like anything else," says Altman. "And eventually you start working on it and you start building up the ability to do it more and more frequently. And I think that as you do—it's a kind of meta-awareness. So it's an awareness of the body. It's an awareness of the mind. It's a different kind of awareness and you start to know it firsthand. So it's very much experiential. It's very different from talking about it and experiencing it, two very different things. You can talk about what it's like to hit a baseball and what you need to hit a baseball out of the park. It's a very different thing to stand in the batter's box and have that ball come at you at ninety, ninety-five miles an hour and learn how to swing, and that's the skill."

Altman says that mindfulness is an intentional process that enriches the way we interact with others. "Mindfulness gives you a deeper experience of being alive. [It] gives us a deeper feeling of being alive. Mindfulness also helps us create more loving, healthy, and sustainable relationships."

Focus Awareness Outward

Jim Kouzes, a prominent leadership researcher and executive educator, believes that truly self-aware individuals are mindful of what's happening around them. In workshops that Kouzes conducts he often engages participants in self-awareness-building exercises in which they work in groups of two or three. As they interact with one another, Kouzes "asks people to pay attention to self, initially—asking, How are you feeling now? How is your body reacting? Is your stomach tense? Are you nervous?" Then Kouzes shifts the point of view when he asks the participants, "Are you focused on the other person (in your group)? Are you distracted, looking away?" The exercise is simple, but when carried into subsequent rounds, the participants gradually begin to notice more about the other person (or persons) in their group.

Kouzes says that initially participants feel uneasy because this kind of focused observation is different from their normal routine, but "after a few minutes of doing it, [the observation] becomes relatively easy for people." The point is that we can train ourselves to be mindful of our own thoughts and feelings, and we can do the same with others. And, being mindful of the situation around us is critical to developing an ability to connect with others.

It is not easy. As Rich Sheridan, cofounder and CEO of Menlo Innovations, an Ann Arbor–based software firm, notes, "As a leader you're pulled simultaneously in two directions constantly. And I think that is the challenge of leadership. There's that one aspect of leadership that requires the ability to envision a better future than where you're at today and that requires you to lift your head up and look down the road as far as you can." "But that only gets you kind of half the way there because the other part is, what's happening today?" says Sheridan. "What's happening right now? If I lift my head up and only look five miles down the road to try and figure out what's ahead, I'm very likely to stumble. I'm very likely to trip over something that's right in front of me, stub my toe, fall down, skin my knee, or slow down because I'm not paying attention to the stuff that's happening today, right now."

Mark Goulston, MD, a psychiatrist and executive coach, takes the observation to another level. "Noticing is different than watching. Looking or seeing [something] is being completely present and engaged with whatever you're noticing. It is what I call 'interpersonal mindfulness.' "

That is something that Chester Elton, a best-selling author who's been dubbed "the Apostle of Appreciation," would endorse. As Elton says, "I have always appreciated leaders who were not careless in their relationships. And what I mean by that is, and this comes back to being mindful, is that it always bothered me when senior executives would blow off your appointment or would start late or come in late and they were just careless with your time. They didn't get back to people. They didn't keep their appointment. And, of course, the higher up you are, you'd say this guy's the president, this guy's the CEO, he's got a lot of things going on. Yeah, but the message is very clear of what my value is when that leader is careless with my relationship. And I found in particular those were reasons why people leave."

A leader is the public face of his team or organization. As such, the leader is always on stage, so his actions have consequences. Elton says, "Great leaders have to be mindful that their decisions have a ripple effect and that even casual comments can cause huge ripples throughout the organization."

Motivating others, says Elton, is all about being aware of their thoughts and feelings. "Motivating others is all about asking, 'What's most important to you?' Then use [that information] to make sure that happens. For example, for some people their motivation is family. So anything you could do…to get them home earlier or let them take a spouse on a trip, works really well. Other people are just ridiculously ambitious, so you couldn't give them enough work and want to do as much as they can to be noticed." Sheridan provides a good example of being mindful of the here and now and what it means to people and the organization. For example, as Sheridan notes, he found dirty dishes in the office's kitchen sink. "Why am I paying attention to that? Because to me it's indicative of a team whose members may not be respecting one another by leaving dishes for others to clean. And as the leader I have to watch for those little things as well because those are the things that will really knock you down over time."

What Sheridan is getting to is what we call situational awareness.

Situational Awareness

Another form of mindfulness is situational awareness. This is knowing where you are and what you need to do next. Those who play sports well typically excel at situational awareness. They know where the opponent is and what they must do to make their play. In games like hockey, soccer, and basketball, players shift constantly from offense to defense and back again, depending upon ball control. The difference between offense and defense is more defined in baseball and football, but once play begins, assigned roles could change in a heartbeat.

Perhaps the game that provides the clearest version of situational awareness is golf. Golfers play the shots they hit. With each stroke, a golfer must consider the angle at which the play rests (the lie), the depth of grass (fairway or rough), and the terrain (sand traps, swales, and trees). Depending upon the conditions, including gauging wind direction, the player chooses the best club for the situation—a driver off the tee, long irons for long fairway shots, and short irons for close-in shots. More importantly, the golfer needs to know his abilities; that is, he needs to know which club is best for his position and his capability. Situational awareness, coupled with self-awareness, is critical to playing well.

Situational awareness is paramount in managerial situations. Managers need to ask themselves what is going on, or not going on, in their departments. The manager needs to know what resources she can share with her team. And most importantly, she needs to evaluate the skills and talents of her team.

The spectrum of available resources—both company resources and team strengths and weaknesses—form the backdrop to situational awareness related to challenges the team is facing as well as the roadblocks it faces. Let's say the team is in human resources and has been asked to develop a new recruitment program. Using the popular SWOT method, managers consider the strengths of the company as well as its weaknesses, including opportunities for growth and threats from inside or outside.

Emerging from this analysis is the knowledge the manager needs to assign the right people to the right jobs, so she can develop a program that targets candidates who will fit the needs of the company now and, perhaps more importantly, in the future.

Understanding the situation comes from asking the right questions. As CEO of Campbell Soup Company, Doug Conant and his team focused on "listening before leading." Doing so is not as easy as it sounds. In the press of business, as Conant explains, executives are pushed to make decisions out of a sense of expediency with "quick judgments." The challenge, as Conant explains, is to slow down and let things settle a bit. Conant is fond of the Stephen Covey mantra "Seek first to understand and then to be understood." Learning the situation then becomes fundamental to developing strong situational awareness.

State of Mindfulness

A good example of situational awareness on a macro-level scale might be Jerry Brown, governor of California at the time of this writing. In the 1970s and '80s, Brown was nicknamed Governor Moonbeam for his big ideas and perhaps also for his lack of organizational prowess in getting them done. With his handsome looks, he dated A-list celebrities like Linda Ronstadt and Natalie Wood. But by the mid-1980s, Brown's political career seemed to be over, and he was viewed as an afterthought.

Now in his mid-seventies, Brown is serving his second stint

as governor (in his third term) and *Bloomberg Businessweek* dubbed him in a 2013 cover story "The Real Terminator." The title refers to Brown's success in reducing California's debt and restoring its fiscal integrity. (His predecessor, Arnold Schwarzenegger, was unable to achieve those results.) Brown's fiscal mastery, as detailed in *Bloomberg Businessweek* by Joel Stein, involves demonstrating the problem to the electorate and then dramatizing the effect of the failure to act.[7] The more you think about it, the more remarkable the transformation becomes—Brown, a man well-known for his liberal political positions who could have made many happy by sniping from the sidelines, stepped up when he thought no one else could.

Brown's rescue plan was born of crisis. When he took office in 2011, the state was $27 billion in debt and had the worst credit rating of all fifty states, according to Standard & Poor's. Unemployment was 12.4 percent. California was in rough water. Brown leveraged this proverbial burning platform to look for solutions that would avert catastrophe.[8]

Longtime friend actor Warren Beatty said, "Since he has been chief executive of [California] twice, he has achieved a level of wisdom about the realities of the various conflicting forces that very few people have been able to achieve." Such awareness comes from Brown's deep intellect (he entered a Jesuit seminary, though was not ordained, and has studied Buddhism) and his commitment to doing things that matter now. Brown made deep cuts to social programs that antagonized liberals, but he also raised taxes slightly, irritating conservatives.[9]

In 2013, unemployment dropped to 9.4 percent and the state posted a surplus of $850 million. California still faces a huge pension liability of more than $77 billion for state employees, so there is work to be done, but septuagenarian Brown views his role as one that entails creating a path to the future by doing

things differently. Or, as he says, "There has to be drama…
we're on the stage of history."[10]

As lofty a role as Brown sees for himself, he harkens back to
his great-grandfather, August Schuckman, who migrated to California in the 1850s. A rock from the property Brown inherited
sits on the coffee table in his modestly adorned office. Brown
says, "When [Schuckman] came out here, you got your hands
in the dirt, you got some people to work with you." That is the
approach Brown applies to fixing California, one that is more
people-centric than "state-centric."[11] Such practicality affirms
Brown's grounded approach to governance.

Brown, like Mandela, is a mindful soul. In our exploration of mindfulness, we can see how these leaders use it to their
advantage—to awaken people to an issue and then find ways to
stir them to take positive action.

Situational awareness is essential to leadership, because it
focuses the leader's attention on what is happening. More specifically, it focuses the leader's attention on what is happening
with the team. In my career, I have seen leaders go out of their
way to keep in touch with their people, whether they are across
the hall or across an ocean. They know it's essential to listen and
learn how other people see issues, and also to understand how
they process work flow, tackle challenges, and achieve success.

"No plan survives first contact with the enemy," wrote Prus-
sian general Helmuth von Moltke. Echoes of this thought have
been put in many different forms because it captures the challenge that leaders face when they act upon their ideas or their
strategies. "Work the plan" means more than follow directions,
it means observe what is happening, listen to what people are
saying, and then change accordingly, if necessary. A mindful
leader will put himself into a position where he can watch what's
happening and listen to what others are saying.

Mindful Leadership

In Steven Spielberg's *Lincoln*, the opening scene features President Lincoln (played by Daniel Day-Lewis) on a battlefield somewhere in the rain listening to what black soldiers are saying. Whether this exact scene ever occurred, it was typical of Lincoln, a humble man, to meet with soldiers as well as the common folks (as he was one himself) to listen to their stories and gauge from their words how they thought about the war or issues of the day.[12]

Ryan Lance, CEO of ConocoPhillips, the world's largest independent exploration and production company, is noted for the time he spends with his employees. Throughout his career, starting out of high school as a roustabout and roughneck on oil rigs, Lance has used interaction with fellow employees to learn the oil and gas business at every level. Today as CEO, he regularly visits facilities throughout the world, from Alaska's North Slope to Australia's gas fields near Brisbane. He considers these visits a form of mindful leadership. "It's a way to really take stock of the situation before you react or make a decision."

Additionally, mindful leaders share their presence. That is, they let people know who they are and what they stand for. "I think most people want leaders who don't overreact and aren't impulsive," says Lance. "If you want to stay in touch with the pulse of the company, you need to know what's really going on. You need to hear what people tell you, but then you also need to know what's going on behind the scenes. I believe that good leaders have that sense of calm, or what I refer to as quiet confidence, and most people want this from a leader. So mindfulness is a trait of that quiet confidence."

For a busy executive, mindfulness requires practice and

adherence to principle. As Lance says, "You're always going to get pressure to deviate from your strategic intentions. You have to be mindful of the elements of the present situation that are trying to distract you from the strategic vision or objectives you have in mind, and you really have to provide a sense of consistency for the organization. They need to see that you're still executing relative to your strategic objections, even as you react to the current day-to-day changes in the business environment."

Mindful Future

Psychiatrist and executive coach Mark Goulston references a quote by famous psychoanalyst Wilfred Bion, who said, "To be present is to listen without memory or desire." What Bion meant, as Goulston explains, "is that when you listen with memory you have an old personal agenda and you're trying to plug people into it. And when you listen with desire you have a new personal agenda that you're trying to plug people into, but you're not really in touch with them."

Mindful leaders do not have agendas, according to Goulston. They focus their messages and themselves on a vision and mission for the organization that is so compelling and appealing that it enrolls people spontaneously, and they want to serve that. Toward that end, Goulston favors what he calls "moon mission." Borrowing from President John F. Kennedy's call to action, Goulston says, "A moon mission has four components. The first is there has to be a date to it . . . as Kennedy said, before the end of the decade. Second, it has to be something that people can visualize. We're going to put them on the moon and get them back. Third, it has to be a grand idea. And fourth, it has to be impossible right now."

Power to Persevere

Mindfulness shapes a leader's character. And, when called upon, leaders put their character into action. A stunning example of such character is the story of Judith Tebbutt, a British mental health social worker, who was captured by Somali pirates in September 2011 while on holiday in Kenya. Her husband was killed, but Tebbutt was used as a bargaining chip for ransom. Her memoir of the experience, *A Long Walk Home*, details how she kept physically and mentally active during her six-month captivity. In an interview with Dan Damon of BBC World Service she detailed how she persevered. Tebbutt said she wrote *A Long Walk Home* to provide inspiration for other hostages: "Do not give up hope, you haven't been forgotten." The lessons she shares, however, are applicable to anyone seeking to hold onto their values and convictions in the face of poor odds.[13]

Tebbutt considered herself fit, so when she was first put into what she termed "the Big House," where she was held captive, she paced out the dimensions of her room and walked her room on schedule—every half hour during daylight. She also did Pilates, to the dismay of her captors.

Tebbutt also engaged her mind. She sat regularly on her bed and imagined herself driving through the countryside in Cumbria, the part of England where she is from. She was given a small radio, which she used to listen to BBC World Service. "I was sitting in a very dark room listening to you," she told reporter Dan Damon. "You have no idea what that means to me."

Part of her strategy was to learn some of the Somali language so she could communicate: "Even though I despised these people, I knew that if I was going to be in their company for any length of time, I needed to try and build a rapport with them."

She also smiled at them. Her guards tried to make her wear full Somali dress, and when she did for the first time they complimented her as "Beauty Somali woman." Tebbutt rebelled and did not acquiesce, adopting only the hijab. "I felt suffocated covered in all these robes," she said.

Identity is critical to self-preservation. Tebbutt cautions that you cannot "lose your own identity. However cruel they are to you, however they degrade you, you must remind yourself of who you are all the time. I was still Jude." During her captivity Tebbutt was also looking forward. "I wanted to come out [of captivity] as Jude. I wanted to find a life for Jude again." Even though she lost her husband tragically and was deprived of her liberty, Tebbutt is not consumed by a need for revenge. "I don't want [my captors] to have power over me." Therefore she thinks of them on her own terms—when she wants to, not because she must.

The experience that Tebbutt endured is an extreme example, but her lessons in mindfulness serve to remind us that we can, when we apply ourselves, keep our minds active even in hardship. Such a lesson is important to remember because leaders face hardships daily, and while most of these hardships are not physically threatening, they feel overwhelming. The challenge is to keep mentally sharp and do as Tebbutt did—maintain perspective on the situation. It was a strategy that enabled her to endure and it can help leaders adapt.

Mindfulness is an approach to leadership in which the leader is focused not only on the moment, but also on the people in that moment who will affect the future of the organization. Mindful leaders are engaged and their engagement sets the example for others to follow.

Mindful Intentions

Situational awareness, as we saw with Lincoln, is a matter of engaging with others. However, it involves more than people-engagement. It requires an ability to engage one's own self. Again, Lincoln serves as a good example of a man in touch with himself. Although he was deeply fatalistic (and had premonitions of his own death), he knew what he was capable of doing. His humility was dumbfounding at times. As we know from Doris Kearns Goodwin's biography *Team of Rivals*, Lincoln peopled his cabinet with political figures who had opposed him. He admired the talents of these men and knew that the only hope of repairing a divided nation was to bring people, including those who disagreed with him, together to work for a common cause—the healing of the Union.[14]

Lincoln's ability to tolerate dissent and to work with people who were his enemies was rooted in his character (we will explore more about character in chapter 3). "Mindfulness is very much rooted in character," says Donald Altman. "Actually, if you go back to the ancient history of mindfulness, you will find the four foundations of mindfulness. One of those foundations is ethics and values." For Altman, mindfulness helps us re-invigorate our values because it helps us live and lead more intentionally and more purposefully. According to Altman, "Companies have mission statements about what's important to them. And as individuals we need to have intention statements for our careers, intention statements for friendships, for our personal health, and our emotional well-being. When intentionality is connected to our values it becomes our personalized steering wheel. It helps turn us in the direction that we want to go. And if we're getting off track in some way, our sense of intention will help guide us back."

Altman suggests that individuals develop a three- or four-sentence intention statement. He invites people to ask themselves: "Do you want to have a career where you are open with others, producing something of value, showing respect, putting in the best effort you can in that job?" While the process can be time-consuming, it helps focus the mind and spirit on greater goals. As a reminder of intention, Altman suggests, "Have people carry that intention statement with them and to see are your actions—are your daily behaviors and actions consistent with that three- or four-sentence intention statement?" Mindfulness rests upon a foundation of intention, a willingness to look at the present with the commitment to make things better for others. Mindful leaders are cognizant of their own shortcomings but also have the humility to acknowledge them and the street smarts to leverage their strengths.

Closing Thought: Mindfulness

While mindfulness originates from within the individual, the practice of it puts the individual, in particular the leader, front and center of what is happening in the here and now, and it helps her focus on what may come in the future. A mindful leader is aware of the situation as well as of how people on her team will react to that situation. As such, a mindful leader is vigilant but also attuned to the inevitable forces of change. Mindfulness, then, prepares leaders to focus on the present as well as prepare for the future.

Mindfulness = Awareness + Intention

Leadership Questions

- What gets you up in the morning and why?
- How do you prepare yourself to engage with the world?
- How often do you make time to ask yourself what is happening, what is not happening, and what you can do to influence the outcome?
- How well are you succeeding at doing what you enjoy most?
- What will you do differently to ensure that you keep working at your best?
- Are you making time to reflect on what you have done? What are your thoughts about what is working and what is not working? What changes will you make?

Leadership Directives

- When you are mindful, you must be fully in the moment. Mindfulness commits you to being fully aware, fully engaged, fully committed.
- Identify what you like to do, what you are good at doing personally and professionally. Consider why you like doing these things.
- Make a list of the things you like about your work. Be as specific as you can.
- Make a list of things you do not like about your work. Be as specific as you can.
- Understand that what you like about work may be the hardest thing that you do, but from it comes the greatest satisfaction.
- Look for inspiration in the actions of those you admire. Ask yourself how they do it and how that might apply to you.

2

Opportunity

The biggest human temptation is to settle for too little.
THOMAS MERTON

Making the Break

Chester Elton, best-selling author dubbed the "Apostle of Appreciation," and his business partner Adrian Gostick had been colleagues at a previous employer. In the last year of their employment at that company, things did not go well. As Elton explains, "I consider us not being able to figure out how to stay with our past employer and still be productive as a huge failure. We should have been able to communicate better and work together in a more productive way. But we couldn't find a way forward. No matter how hard we worked or how much success we had, we couldn't make our bosses happy or find happiness ourselves."

Elton credits his wife, Heidi, with providing him with the support he needed to go out on his own. According to Elton, "She said, 'Look, I know you're really struggling with leaving. You are a loyal guy. You love the company, but a company can't love you back! Let me make this simple for you . . . you're leaving. Let's just figure out how.' And the reason she said that is because, 'This job is killing you. It's literally killing you. I want my husband back. The kids want their dad back. So you're leaving. Now, let's just figure out how we're gonna do that.'" That's what a great spouse does for you.

Elton realized that he had to make a move. "Leaving is never easy, especially after nineteen years. But things change, leaders change, and you can't always make the change. No one is to blame. I still have great friends there and their leader is a genuinely good man. It just wasn't the right place for me anymore. It was time to move."

The challenge of independence beckoned. "And yet the opportunity for us to be on our own and to create our own business, The Culture Works, has been so rewarding and so much fun and so engaging and so profitable. It was one of those things where I thought, 'Geez, if I knew you could do this on your own I would have done this two or three years earlier.'"

Failure is not the end. "I think when you talk to people who are success driven, they really do look at those failures as 'Here's where we are now. Now what do we do?' We can cry. We can laugh. We can stew in our juices or we can pick ourselves up and move along. And my response to failure has always been to just work harder. You just work harder, and the harder you work the luckier you get and the more success you have."

Making the Most of Serendipity

In a recent conversation, Jim Kouzes, professor and author, told me his story of opportunities and serendipitous events. "My entire career has been a series of serendipitous events. I seem to have had accidental encounters with opportunities, and I guess I've been both lucky and smart enough to take advantage of each.

For example, right out of university I joined the Peace Corps, and I was assigned to teach. I had no idea at the time how much I would enjoy teaching. I thought I wanted to be a Foreign Service officer. But when I got back to the U.S. I decided that I wanted to get a job in teaching."

After three years working for the Community Action Training Institute, Kouzes was recruited by the School of Social Work at San Jose State University to run a grant project that provided training to mental health administrators in the San Francisco Bay area. That led to a job directing the Executive Development Center at Santa Clara University, which is where Kouzes met his eventual coauthor and business partner, Barry Posner.

"Barry knocked on my door the first day I was there in my new office at Santa Clara and said, 'You're in my office.' I was initially surprised and said, 'What? I thought the dean told me this was my office.' Then he laughed and said, 'Well, it *is* your office now, but it was my office.' Then Barry said, 'Since you're new to campus, just let me know how I can help. If there's anything you need I'd be glad to show you around. I also do some work with the Executive Development Center, and if there's anything I can do to help out there let me know.' And I said, 'Great.' I took advantage of that opportunity, and the result has been a rewarding three-decade collaboration. I learned two lessons from that early connection with Barry—and from all my other serendipitous encounters. First, knock on more doors. Knock on lots of doors. Second, always say yes when somebody asks, 'Can I help?' Yes is the only word that starts things."

RESEARCH SAYS...

OF TOP 20 COMPANIES FOR LEADERSHIP, RESPONDENTS SAY THAT:

90%

SENIOR LEADERS
COMMUNICATE THE
URGENCY OF THEIR
FIRM ADAPTING TO
EVOLVING MARKET
TRENDS

70%

ENCOURAGE
EMPLOYEES TO
LEARN IN AREAS
OUTSIDE THEIR
AREAS OF EXPERTISE

SOURCE: 2013 BEST COMPANIES FOR LEADERSHIP HAY GROUP[1]

Opportunity. Individuals with moxie do not wait for things to come to them. They seek new opportunities. They are seekers of the new and different.

Ben Hogan

When asked the secret of his success, this phenom used to say as if it were a secret, that "It was in the dirt." Many have speculated about what he meant by that, but on the surface it meant that you had to do the work. He was a golfer and he spent hour after hour hitting golf balls off the grass and the dirt. But it went deeper. Dirt for him represented the determination that he brought to his game. Short in stature, his compact frame was wiry and muscled, unlike the lean lankiness of other golfers of his generation. Whatever power he generated could come from his arms, shoulders, torso, hips, and legs. And it is the latter two that gave him the most trouble. But it is the reason that he is revered to this day. He was Ben Hogan, champion golfer.

Born in Texas to impoverished parents, young Hogan learned the game at a country club near Fort Worth where he caddied. In those days, professional golf was hardly a profession at all; it was more akin to a group of itinerant gamblers rolling from town to town to compete for prize money that totaled little more than a few thousand dollars. Still, something about the game appealed to Hogan, and he decided to make it his career.

Nothing came easy to him. His first years on the tour were nothing spectacular, but he did win a few tournaments. During World War II, he served in the Army Air Corps and trained as a pilot. He never went overseas. Stationed in his native Texas, Hogan and had time, like other golfers in this era, to work on his game. It was after the war that he began to make a reputation, winning a number of tournaments including the U.S. Open and the PGA Tournament, known in professional golf as "the majors."

But an event in 1949 defined Hogan's life and ultimately made him the icon he is today. Driving home to Texas from a tournament in Los Angeles, a bus swerved into his lane and pancaked his new Buick and his legs. At the last moment, Hogan swung himself out from behind the steering wheel to shield his wife from the impact. By doing so he likely not only saved her from injury, but also prevented himself from being crushed by the onrushing steering column. Unfortunately, his legs were in the path of impact and they were mangled so severely that it was first reported that Hogan had perished in the accident.

Talk of Hogan walking again seemed premature. But during the long months in the hospital and then at home in recovery he resolved not only to walk again but to play golf. Somewhere in the back of his mind he resolved also to compete. Although shy and reserved, Hogan had built up a reservoir of goodwill among his fellow golfers, tournament officials, and even sportswriters. He was selected as the captain of the American team that traveled to Scotland in 1949 to play in the Ryder Cup. He did not compete but he led the winning team.

Perhaps it was being back in the golf world that tempted him to try again professionally. Upon returning to Fort Worth, he began hitting balls for hours on end. Then, in 1950, he pronounced himself ready enough and entered the Los Angeles Open, held at Riviera Country Club. He hit the course like a whirlwind, scoring well enough to place in the money, though it was difficult. His legs swelled upon walking, let alone playing golf, and they ached painfully during the four rounds of competition.

But it is what happened six months later that launched Hogan into golf history. He entered the U.S. Open at Merion Country Club outside Philadelphia. The U.S. Open is regarded by many as the toughest tournament of all; the course is typically rigged to be challenging, and it attracts the best of the best players. Hogan had won the 1948 U.S. Open, but that was on two good legs. Now he was hobbled, but he gave it his all.

As Dave Barrett explained in *Miracle at Merion*, the tournament took place only sixteen months after the crippling accident. Hogan willed himself around the course, playing thirty-six holes to seal a playoff berth then another eighteen the next day. Red Smith, legendary New York sportswriter, wrote, "Maybe once in a lifetime...it is possible to say with accuracy and without mawkishness, 'This was a spiritual victory, an absolute triumph of will.' This is that one time."[2]

The 1950 U.S. Open was Ben Hogan's moment. It was at Merion that he established himself as a player who defied the odds and used a combination of guts and guile to win. Hogan had confidence that he would and could do well. He had prepared himself to compete at the highest level and he did. This was Ben Hogan's moment and he played to a tee.[3]

*****

Seizing the moment is what Ben Hogan did and what leaders who succeed do. Opportunities, as the adage goes, come to those who seek them. And that is critical for a leader. Few, if any, are content to sit back and wait for things to happen. They look for windows of opportunity where they can apply what they know and do to what needs doing. They are opportunistic in mind-set, and their need to succeed drives them to take advantage of what happens next.

Facing Adversity

Opportunity also requires perseverance. Max De Pree, former chairman and CEO of furniture maker Herman Miller as well as an author, once wrote, "The first responsibility of a leader is to define reality. The last is to say thank you. In between you become a servant and a debtor." Jim Kouzes uses that quote to get to the heart of a leader's responsibility—to tell the truth.

That truth begins with a look inward. In his more than

thirty years of research, including collecting best practice stories for *The Leadership Challenge* (now in its fifth edition), Kouzes notes that nearly every story featured offers an example of someone facing a significant challenge. "One of the things that was striking about this—and not something we expected—was that every single story was about challenge, adversity, uncertainty, difficulty, and change. It wasn't about maintaining the status quo. No one ever did their best by keeping things the same. Every situation was about changing the way things were—and often very dramatically." Some folks climbed mountains; others started businesses; and still others rebuilt them.

Inherent in facing adversity is a willingness to look beyond the immediate problem to see possibilities over the horizon. One of Kouzes's favorite quotes is from legendary Hollywood agent and deal maker Swifty Lazar, who said, "Sometimes I wake up in the morning and there's nothing doing so I make something happen by lunch." Kouzes likes to tell leaders to "Post this quote on your wall or computer screen so you can remind yourself to take initiative. Every day when lunchtime arrives if you haven't made something happen, delay lunch." That's where opportunity enters.[4]

Leveraging Adversity

We can also view opportunity as the flip side of adversity. Doug Conant discovered this when he was named CEO of Campbell Soup Company in 2001. Although he was a veteran of the food industry, having worked for General Mills, Kraft, and Nabisco, nothing prepared him for the challenges he would face at Campbell Soup. The first eighteen months were tough. He realized that the challenges facing the company were beyond the scope of its leaders. As Conant said, "You can't talk yourself out of something you behaved your way into. You have to behave your way out of it."

The approach Conant implemented was methodical. Using a three-year plan, he challenged executives to develop annual operating plans and quarterly priorities. Nothing special there, but Conant insisted in the first year that such plans and priorities be reviewed by his executive team via e-mail every Friday and subsequently discussed in a Monday morning staff meeting. Attendance was mandatory. "It was a very disciplined process [focused] on getting control of the enterprise and getting it on firmer footing."

That sounds good, but it also requires the personal commitment of those at the top. And in this regard Conant found himself doubly challenged: he was new to Campbell and he was an introvert, the quiet and reserved type. However, he realized that if he was going to turn Campbell around he would have to be highly visible. So, early in his tenure, he discussed his introversion publicly, or, as he says now, he declared himself. Specifically, he told his employees, "You are going see me standing off to the side [at some corporate event] and you may think of me as aloof and not interested in who you are and what you are doing." But that's not the whole story. "The reality is I'm just shy and I don't know what to say." Conant asked others to make conversation with him, and it worked. "It took the weight of the world off my shoulders as a leader," he said. Admitting such shyness enabled him to focus on his job and at the same time it invited others to converse, and, more importantly, to communicate with him honestly and directly. Over time, Conant's shyness dissipated because he had "stopped internalizing it."

As important as a structured turnaround is, it cannot work without making changes. "I had to create a culture of creativity and accountability," says Conant, because "99 percent of decisions made within a company are being made when [the

CEO] is not in the room." Under Conant's tenure, Campbell expanded its soup product line to meet the needs of consumers who wanted to eat soup at work or on the go. "We were always on the lookout for new and better ways to do things," he said. Driving the turnaround plan, as well as creative impulses, was a sense of urgency: "We had to innovate or die." Building on that was the mantra, "the number one expectation of a leader was to inspire the trust of others."

Not every executive was up to the task, and the company replaced more than 300 of the top 350 executives. One hundred fifty of these were hired externally, but another 150 or so were promoted from within. These folks "were dying to contribute in a more substantial way but weren't given the opportunity," Conant found. These executives rose to the challenge, and after three years Campbell was back on top, posting a solid performance for the next eight years of Conant's tenure.

Making Things Happen: Three Case Studies

Creating opportunity is often a matter of looking in the right place at the right time. Consider McDonald's big hit of 2013— the McWrap. McDonald's is the global behemoth in fast food. Introducing new products that are extensions of existing products, be they hamburgers or chicken sandwiches, is not that difficult. Introducing a new line of food that is fresh, appealing to the health-conscious, and can be made simply, cost effectively, and quickly is another matter.

According to a *Bloomberg Businessweek* cover story, McDonald's spent fourteen months working on the McWrap. Don Thompson, CEO of McDonald's, summed up the challenge aptly when asked about the changing taste preferences of younger consumers: "We're as vulnerable today as we always have been. Tastes have been changing." So finding opportunity is not a nice thing to do; it's a strategic imperative.

Failure to change may cost the company customers, and launching a product that fails can be embarrassing as well as costly. The Arch Deluxe, a hamburger launched in 1996, cost $100 million to introduce. It bombed and then disappeared. So introducing a new product can be a roll of the dice.

The idea for the McWrap was not a made-in-America story. A version of a chicken wrap first appeared in McDonald's Poland. Unlike other fast food companies that push for homogeneity in their offerings across the world, McDonald's has a long history of adapting its menus to suit local tastes. In a sense, it's an extension of founder Ray Kroc's approach to letting owner–operators develop new product ideas. The Big Mac and Egg McMuffin are two such examples.

Assembling the right ingredients at the right price point in ways that appeal to American taste buds was a long journey that began in the head chef's test kitchen. Ingredients that made the final cut, in addition to chicken, were cucumber, cheese, sauce (squiggled, not poured), and a white flour tortilla. Time and consumers' taste preferences will determine the product's future, but the exercise in new product development is a solid case study of mobilizing a company to deliver what consumers might be interested in. Note the words "might be." After all, when Henry Ford was quizzed about customer intention a century ago, he reportedly quipped, "If I had asked my customers what they wanted, they would have said, 'A faster horse.'" Opportunity can be serendipitous but it must be pursued.[5]

While McDonald's is seeking to respond to consumer shifts in food preference, another company is seeking to deliver on the need for zero-emission vehicles. Enter Elon Musk, a billionaire entrepreneur who has turned the electric car into a thing of desire—high desire. The Tesla electric cars are favorites of Hollywood celebrities as well as the rich and famous.

Tesla Motors, unlike other companies that make only electric cars, is profitable. One reason may be the car's roots. It was developed by non-car guys who were more into technology than mobility, and their approach focused on battery functionality. Today, a top-end Tesla has a range of three hundred miles, more than any other electric vehicle. Quick charging is another feature—twenty minutes can replenish the battery so it's good for another two hundred miles. Other electric models require hours of recharging. Styling is also appealing, and, unlike other carmakers, Tesla controls its retail outlets. No franchise dealers. This enables concierge-like service and innovative financing plans.

Tesla's business does not rival that of Ford or Toyota, but it does demonstrate that savvy entrepreneurs can deliver on opportunities if they can marshal the right resources for their dreams. Elon Musk, who made his fortune as a cofounder of PayPal, is the right guy to capitalize on opportunities to deliver value to customers and profits to company coffers. His other major venture is SpaceX, a company that is pioneering privately financed space travel. In May 2012, one of his rockets docked with the International Space Station.[6]

One established company and one entrepreneurial start-up are demonstrating that strong leaders find opportunities where change meets need. Capitalizing on this intersection requires an ability to communicate the vision to others and to mobilize them to execute it in ways that deliver value.

Opportunities often arise from disruption. Disruption can be an effective strategy when it comes to doing something different and making it work to build a business. One example is Netflix, which has disrupted the marketplace not once but multiple times. As TV critic David Carr noted in a perceptive column for the *New York Times*, Netflix first disrupted video distribution by using the U.S. Post Office as its distributor of DVDs. This effort was immensely popular and the business grew.[7]

Then Netflix began streaming video directly to subscribers, who paid a monthly service fee that entitled them to watch as many movies or TV shows per month as they wished. Again, the business model proved successful.

The next disruption was self-inflicted. In August 2011, Netflix decided to split the businesses into two different business units, meaning customers needed to pick which service to use or pay 60 percent more to keep both. The outcry was huge and Netflix lost as many as one-third of its subscriber base. CEO Reed Hastings, who had been recognized by *Fortune* magazine as CEO of the Year in 2010, looked to have made a huge mistake.

But, as Forbes.com commentator Adam Hartung wrote, "CEO Hastings actually did what textbooks tell us to do— he began milking the installed, but outdated, DVD business. He did not kill it, but he began pulling profits and cash out of it to pay for building the faster growing, but lower margin, streaming business." And it worked. The streaming business grew and the DVD business declined.[8]

It was now time for its third disruption—creating exclusive content for Netflix. The first major effort was the funding of twenty-six episodes of a Netflix-only series, *House of Cards*, a political drama starring Kevin Spacey as an ambitious politician on the make. The first thirteen episodes were launched in spring of 2013 and the response was hugely positive. The practice of releasing all new episodes at once was again disruptive and validated a trend that many viewers had already adopted—binge viewing, watching one series in large doses.

House of Cards is a bona fide hit and garnered a number

of Emmy nominations. And as TV critic and media professor
David Bianculli told David Carr, "It took HBO twenty-five years
to get its first Emmy nomination; it took Netflix six months."[9]

Netflix subsequently resurrected a network TV show,
Arrested Development, that had been canceled four years
earlier. It also introduced a couple of other shows of its own,
including *Orange Is the New Black,* a drama set in a women's
prison. The content-creation model was working.

Nothing Netflix did was extraordinary per se, but by
looking at what consumers wanted in terms of television watching, it was able to deliver movies and TV shows directly, first
through the mail and later via the Internet. Creating its own
content was the next huge step, and it shows that innovation
need not be totally original; rather, it must be focused on providing something different in terms of convenience.[10]

Taking Opportunity to the Next Level

Successful leaders capitalize on opportunities, but they do something more. They create opportunities for others. The greatest
untapped reservoir of organizational strength is purpose. That
statement is a definition I have often used when I speak and
write about the power of purpose. And so when I read, "The
greatest untapped source of motivation is a sense of service to
others," my brain blinked *Bingo*!

The quote comes from a *New York Times Magazine* profile
by Susan Dominus about the work of Adam Grant, a thirty-one-
year old professor at Wharton. Grant has published a slew of
peer-reviewed papers and is the author of a new book, *Give and
Take: A Revolutionary Approach to Success.* The rest of the
quote, which is Dominus's summary of Grant's thinking, notes
that when we as employees consider our "contribution of work

to other people's lives [it has] the potential to make us more productive than thinking about ourselves."[11]

Grant, who was interviewed for the article, says, "In corporate America, people do sometimes feel that the work they do isn't meaningful. And contributing to coworkers can be a substitute for that." Grant's research proves his thesis. Employees are more engaged and motivated when they feel they are contributing beneficially to others.

Grant himself models this behavior. According to the *New York Times Magazine*, he views teaching and advising students—even those not enrolled at Wharton whom he encounters via email—as part of his job, not something extra. It does not hinder his productivity; it may indeed improve it.

Essentially, what Grant is documenting, as others have before him, is the power of altruism. As research shows, altruism may be embedded in our DNA; it sparks the impulse to give and take care of others. It certainly sparks volunteerism. People are motivated to help others because they want to, and they feel good about doing so.

In my interview with Grant for this book, he said, "Many leaders underestimate the power of operating like a giver." It is different from charitable giving and volunteerism. "The giver mind-set is a focus on making other people better off.... There is compelling evidence that when leaders operate like givers they do better and so do their organizations." As Grant explains, "Many employees respond to giving leaders by acting like givers themselves, which means more knowledge sharing, more creativity and innovation, and more helping and problem solving." This is beneficial for the organization. What's more, Grant says, "people want to work for someone who puts their interests first." And it makes sense. When we do for others, they may be inclined to do for us. And, as Grant explains, organizations "end up building a culture where it's harder for people to act

like takers and get away with it. You end up...weeding out
these zero-sum games where one employee wins at the expense
of another."

But, as Grant notes, leaders who give and give can wind up
being taken advantage of. So he advises leaders to align their
giving with their "organization's values and goals...Help[ing]
people who are not aligned [with company goals] is a recipe
for disaster." Therefore, you prioritize. Share your expertise
where you can do the most good. That is, if you have expertise
in finance, share that. If your expertise is in human resources,
spread that knowledge. Finally, Grant believes that boundaries
are important. Leaders can and must make time for themselves
to think and reflect as a means of getting their own work done.

Practicing service is another matter, and what makes Grant's
conclusions so powerful is that he is focusing on organizations,
including the corporate sector. Purposeful organizations deliver
on the service equation, both internally and externally. So how
can we show service in the workplace? First and foremost, consider not so much what you do but the outcome of what you do.
That is, think, "What effect will doing my job well have on my
coworkers?" Next, put your mind-set in place. Consider these
options.

Listen, don't judge. Frankly, this might be the toughest advice,
because we often think we know what colleagues will say before
they actually say it. So, rather than preemptively dismissing a
comment, keep an open mind and use this flexible stance as a
point of leverage for conversation. Ask an open-ended question
or ask the person to expand on his comment.

Think "want to" rather than "have to." We all have must-do
tasks. Thinking of them as things you want to do to help another

person perform her job better reframes the work as a matter of helping, not simply completing.

Put benefits before tasks. Look for ways to turn what you do into things that benefit your colleagues. For example, if you finish a task early, you have time to help a coworker. Or if someone is waiting on your decision, an early response helps him initiate a project earlier.

Adopt a "me-last" approach. Marine officers have a tradition of waiting till the junior ranks have been served before they eat. It makes a positive impression when you, as a senior person, defer to a subordinate. It shows that you have respect for others and a sense of humility about yourself.

Step out of the limelight. Let others get credit for a team effort when things go right. And if the reverse occurs, stand up for your team.

These suggestions are intended as thought starters. What you do is up to you, and once you let your mind think more freely you will come up with ways that you can make a difference. So let me share a story.

Once I was working with an executive who had been targeted to move up. The only problem was that at times he would rub his colleagues the wrong way. He would act impatiently, cut people off, and sometimes behave gruffly. That's not uncommon in managers, but here's what was different. This executive was terrific with customers. Whenever there were problems, he was the first person brought in. He was patient, attentive, and understanding, not to mention technically proficient. His behavior with customers was exactly the opposite of his behavior with colleagues.

In our initial coaching conversation, I challenged him to think of his colleagues as his customers. From the look on his face I could tell he made the connection almost instantly. And that was it. He adopted a customer-service mentality toward colleagues, which confirmed his good nature, and people responded better.

Of course, the spirit of giving back, of being of service to others, must be rooted in competence. You must prepare yourself to do your work by being educated and trained. You must do what the job entails and more when it makes a positive difference, as it often does when you see the results your work has on others.

Service is the dividend of purpose. Service validates and renews purpose in ways that make it meaningful for individuals, because it affirms their contributions and strengthens organizations by promoting engagement. By focusing on service, we create opportunities not only for others but for ourselves as well. Service opens the door to deliver on opportunity because it enables the leader to do her job—to work through others to achieve intended goals.

Opportunism: An Entrepreneur's Story

Entrepreneurs are prime examples of opportunists. As Daniel Isenberg, business school professor and best-selling author, argues in his book *Worthless, Impossible, and Stupid,* innovation is not as important as finding the right opportunities.

In a chapter called "Solving Burning Problems," Isenberg creates a word equation that I find pertinent: "Entrepreneurship = adversity + human capital." In short, Isenberg states that problems or challenges present those who are looking to make a difference with the opportunity to create something. All it takes is the problem and some investment capital.[12]

One example that Isenberg profiles is Vinod Kapur, founder of Keggfarms, one of the oldest poultry breeding farms in India. After economic liberalism hit India in 1991, Kapur realized that he could avoid going head to head with global poultry producers since those producers focused on major cities. Kapur found new opportunity in rural India, where 75 percent of the population lives. This population is also extremely poor, so he would have to find a means to grow the business and at the same time help the local populace.

After years of experimentation, Keggfarms introduced the Kerbroiler, a beautifully colored bird (Indians believe white chickens are inferior) that could live on household scraps and that was aggressive enough to fend off local predators, such as dogs. It also added weight quickly and could begin laying eggs by six months. Kerbroilers reached full weight at a year and could be used for meat or kept as egg producers.

Distribution was challenging because it meant distributing perishable items in high heat throughout the rural countryside. The solution was to enlist a network of dealers who would take the one-day-old birds and distribute them to local households once the chicks had achieved a weight of three hundred grams. Each chick costs sixty cents and, because they eat household scraps, they cost nothing to maintain. They lay eggs and can eventually be sold for meat. By solving the breeding issue as well as problems with the distribution system, Keggfarms was able to bring new business opportunities to rural India.[13]

Entrepreneurs are more than problem solvers. They see value where others do not and they can make something out of nothing.[14] Bob Lutz, when he was president of Chrysler, said that one reason Chrysler eyed American Motors was because the company was perennially short of cash but seemed able to continue to produce multiple vehicles. Lutz quipped that sooner or later he would figure out how they could make something out of nothing.

Entrepreneurs learn over time to deal with risk. After all, capitalizing on an idea is a risky venture. Gabi Meron of Given Imaging recognized this when he came across a new technology called PillCam. In essence, it's a swallowable camera that can take pictures of the small intestine. While the obstacles to such a venture, both inside the body as well as outside it (with acceptance and FDA approval) were significant, Meron realized that if he were to bring PillCam to market he would have to think as big as the PillCam was small—that is, he would have to be revolutionary. So he stepped up development of the PillCam and submitted it to the FDA. Given Imaging also rolled out the product in three major markets (the U.S., Europe, and Japan) simultaneously. And it worked. Regulatory approval in Europe came more swiftly than it did in the U.S., so Given Imaging had a revenue stream. And since it was a "proven product" in Europe, the company was able to mitigate risk in Japan by working with local partners.[15]

Hidden Opportunities

While entrepreneurs get much credit, and deservedly so, for perseverance in pursuing opportunities, many successful executives find opportunities in their own organizations, if they look hard enough. Such was the case with Ryan Lance, CEO of ConocoPhillips. Early in his career he was a mid-level manager working for ARCO on Alaska's North Slope. As Lance explains, "We needed to set a new standard for North Slope Arctic developments going forward. Developments needed to be smaller and more sustainable with less environmental impact. And so we set out to create this new standard of excellence."

The challenge was significant, but Lance and his team pursued it: "We put together a conceptual plan to develop the field and took it to ARCO management for approval. They essentially kicked me out and said, 'We like the cost, but don't think you can do this. There are too many technical firsts, too many things you're trying to do at one time, and you'll fail.' So they sent us back to the drawing board. That was a devastating defeat for me and the team."

But, it was not the end. While the team tried alternative plans, none seemed as effective or compelling as their original plan. Lance says, "Two months later we took the exact, identical plan back to management and said, 'This is the way we've got to do it. Give us a chance to prove that we can get it done.' They did approve the project, which put more resolve into the team. We truly believed we had the right answer, the right plan, and we turned that defeat into a victory. In fact, it successfully developed the Alpine Field, which has exceeded all expectations over the course of the last twenty years."

Opportunities fulfilled come to those who pursue them and stick with them even when others may not see its promise of success. Leaders must view opportunity as necessary to moving an organization forward. And when an opportunity fails, a mindful leader will take lessons from the experience and apply it to the next venture.

Closing Thought: Opportunity

Opportunities come to those who seek them and are willing to work hard to make them real, even when the odds of success are formidable. Leaders are mindful of opportunities, but their approach is more than opportunistic. It is holistic. They seek to create opportunities for themselves as well as others.

Opportunities, however, are not pennies from heaven. While sometimes they are the result of serendipitous events, most often they emerge from a combination of awareness and a commitment to discipline. That is, a leader recognizes an idea's potential and then works hard to fulfill it.

Opportunity = Need + Solution

Leadership Questions

- What new opportunities are you looking for and why?
- How well are you succeeding in this search?
- What will you do to ensure that you continue to place yourself in the path of discovering new opportunities?

Leadership Directives

- Look at the opportunities that have come your way in the past two years. How well did you capitalize on them?
- If you did not take advantage of these opportunities, why not? What held you back? What can you do differently to ensure that new opportunities arise?
- An opportunity may come in the form of an invitation to try something new, or it may be as substantial as a new career possibility. It is essential that you clarify each opportunity and consider its merits for you. For example, you may be ready to take on a new assignment at work, but not change careers. On the other hand, you may be ready to go back to school and do something completely different. Clarify your options before you make up your mind.

3

X Factor

Character cannot be developed in ease and quiet. Only through experience of trial and suffering can the soul be strengthened, ambition inspired, and success achieved.

HELEN KELLER

Getting Fired Is Not the Worst Thing

When Doug Conant who later became CEO of Campbell Soup Company was a young executive in his mid-thirties, the division he was working for was spun off. "The new owners came in and decided to eliminate layers of management. In no time I had lost my job. It was an incredibly humbling experience. I was fired in an awkward way. I was devastated and I was bitter...I went home to my wife, my two small children, and my one very large mortgage feeling every bit the victim."

Conant was not the type to give up easily. "I've always believed that if the new owners had wanted to they could have found an opportunity for me, even with the downsizing. They were not particularly invested in my job search. They said, 'Well, you will find another job.' Easy for them to say."

Help is there if we look for it. "The one thing they did that was truly helpful to me was to send me to an executive search person who ultimately became my mentor. He was the one who introduced me to the true meaning behind the words, 'How can I help?' He challenged me to turn the coin over and make the best of a difficult situation. Under his coaching, I was able to move beyond feeling like a victim, to a place where I was proactively advancing my career."

Inspiration comes in different places. "I've always enjoyed reading Louis L'Amour western novels. And in one of his books he had a quote from one of the main characters, 'he never knew when he was licked, so he never was.' That quote inspired the mind-set I learned to bring to my work. If I never felt licked, I really never was. And so I picked myself up and [my executive outplacement counselor] challenged me to run the world's best job search and to pour my energy into that endeavor. I did and it was painful, but productive. It set the table for me to have a good career run after clearly experiencing the most painful job search of my life."

Breakthrough After Breakdown

Mark Goulston is a psychiatrist by training as well as practice. He is also successful executive coach. He appears regularly on television and speaks to thousands in his keynotes and reaches millions through his writing. But his life was not without adversity. "My greatest personal accomplishment over adversity was that I dropped out of medical school twice and finished. I think I was an untreated case of depression and ADHD and the second time I asked for a medical leave, the dean of the school advised the Promotions Committee to ask me to withdraw (since I was passing all my classes), which was a euphemism for being kicked out.

I was at a low point in my life and not able to think very clearly nor able to see any value or future for me."

Fortunately others noticed Mark's plight. "At that point the dean of students, William McNary (Mac), stepped in, and pulled me aside. He believed in me when I couldn't, saw value in me that I didn't, and saw a future for me that I couldn't. The most compelling thing he said to me—and my coming from a rather stern, critical, and negative upbringing you'll truly appreciate it—was, "Mark, even if you don't become a doctor and don't even do much with your life, I'd still be proud to know you, because you have goodness and kindness in you and you have no idea how much the world needs that, and you won't know it until you are thirty-five. The trick is that you have to make it to thirty-five. And one last thing, Mark, and look at me, 'You deserve to be on this planet. Do you understand me?' "

Mark did understand and suddenly Dr. McNary went to bat for him. "Mac appealed my request, which was granted. I went on to do a medical elective at the Menninger Clinic in Topeka and discovered that I could reach schizophrenic farm boys at their Topeka State Hospital, much the way Mac had reached me."

Mark is one who believes in giving back. "And that has been my life's work ever since and what caused me, thirty years after the predicted age of thirty-five, to cofound Heartfelt Leadership where our mission is Daring to Care, just as Mac had done for me."

PERSONALITY ENABLERS
ACCORDING TO DDI'S DATA, EXECUTIVES ASSESS MORE
HIGHLY THAN NON-EXECUTIVES FOR THE FOLLOWING
ATTRIBUTES:

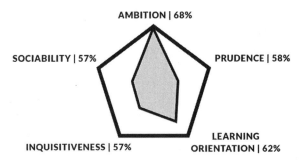

SOURCE: DEVELOPMENTAL DIMENSIONS INTERNATIONAL, INC. 2013[1]

X Factor. Each of us has a unique set of talents and skills that we use to make our way in the world. More than just talent, it includes what makes you—your character, convictions, and personal beliefs. Consider this set the X factor: what enables you to do what you do and do it well. Put simply, X factors form the "right stuff of leadership."

The ultimate measure of a leader's legacy is the effectiveness of her ability to change the situation and leave things in better shape than she found them. If that is the criterion, then certainly Margaret Thatcher stands as a leader to be remembered.

Margaret Thatcher

When Thatcher became prime minister of the United Kingdom in 1979, the country was in turmoil. Many lamented the once proud nation's fall from status. The economy was weak, the trade unions were holding businesses hostage, and arcane rules and regulations hamstrung businesses and threatened the survival of many.

By the time she left office in 1990, the face of Britain had changed. As Alistair MacDonald put in his remembrance of Thatcher for the *Wall Street Journal*, the prime minister was known "for her role in revolutionizing the failing economy"—a process that caused great "social change and division"—as well as for Britain's victory in the Falklands War. "We have ceased to be," Thatcher said after the war," a nation in retreat."

Indeed, retreat was not a word in her vocabulary. "I came to office with one deliberate intent. To change Britain from a dependent to a self-reliant society, from a give-it-to-me to a do-it-yourself nation."

Facing challenge was nothing new to her. Born Margaret Roberts, she attended Oxford and became a research chemist. But politics was in her blood, due in no small part to the influence of her father, Alfred Roberts, who served as mayor of Grantham. He was a grocer, a small businessman, and a Methodist minister who valued free enterprise and gravitated to the Conservative Party.

Margaret Roberts aspired to political office but when she was coming of age in the 1950s, politics in Britain was considered a man's purview. She appealed to party elders for the opportunity to run as the Conservative Party candidate but was turned down. When she finally did earn a spot on the ticket she was defeated twice. By then she had married Denis Thatcher, a globe-trotting oilman, and was the mother of twins, Carol and Mark. She had resigned herself to the idea that elected office was not for her. But when a seat in Finchley, a suburb of London, opened up, she ran and won.

Arriving in Parliament in 1959, she met with resistance and even outright hostility from her male colleagues. Famously, she and Ted Heath, who would later serve as prime minister, were rivals. She would eventually replace him as the leader of the Conservative Party.

Coming to Power

After serving as party leader, Thatcher led the Tories to election victory in 1979 after a winter of national strikes. During her first two years, levels of unemployment rose and the economy shrank. Her prescription was free-market economics, in contrast to the Keynesian model Britain had followed for decades. She was met with stiff resistance, to which she exclaimed, "I am not here to be liked." In time, her measures worked, but the bitterness of those who opposed her remained strong.

Opposition was particularly strong in Northern Ireland. The situation in Northern Ireland had escalated into more terrorism, which at times spread to England and in fact took the life of Airey Neave, one of Thatcher's closest colleagues, prior to her becoming prime minister. At a party conference in 1984 in Brighton, the wife of one of her ministers was killed in a bomb blast and thirty others were injured. The IRA claimed responsibility. Part of the hostility was her refusal to recognize IRA prisoners as political and therefore exempt from regulations governing criminals. IRA prisoners went on a hunger strike and ten died.

She deserves partial credit for opening relations with the Soviet Union. Having met Mikhail Gorbachev before he became president, she noted that he was one with whom "she could do business." She relayed her thoughts to her good friend Ronald Reagan and urged him to reach out to Gorbachev, which he did several times in face-to-face meetings in Geneva and Reykjavík. Upon her death Gorbachev said, "[W]e managed to achieve mutual understanding, and this was a contribution to the changing atmosphere between our country and the West, and to the end of the Cold War."

Margaret Thatcher was a divisive figure. Opponents on the Left disliked her intensely and in fact she helped unite opposition. Her heavy-handed management style also rubbed her Conservative Party colleagues roughly. When, in the end, she was forced from office in what amounted to a party coup, Thatcher shed tears but likely her colleagues shed few. She maintained her equilibrium after someone complained to her that she had been done in by colleagues. "We're in politics, dear," she said.

It's true enough that Thatcher was forced from office by her own party, which had grown tired of her strident management style and her headstrong ways. Yet she had changed the face of Britain, and the prosperity of the 1990s was due in large part to her leadership. She was known as the "Iron Lady," a name that she heartily embraced because it captured her sense of self and her resolute sense of determination.

Twilight Years

Shortly after leaving office in November 1990, Thatcher was elevated to the House of Lords and became known as Baroness Thatcher. She also devoted time to her foundation and occasionally commented on international affairs. In the early 2000s, according to her daughter, Carol, Thatcher was afflicted with dementia, something that was vividly depicted in the movie *The Iron Lady* starring Meryl Streep as Thatcher.

While she could be prickly, she maintained her sense of humor. As MacDonald noted, in 2007 when a bronze statue of her was unveiled in Parliament, she said, "I might have preferred iron, but bronze will do."

After her death, John Burns, a British national who works for the *New York Times*, summed up her legacy on *PBS News Hour* by saying, "The Britain I grew up in, in the wake of the Second World War, was a country which was in precipitous decline, which had entirely lost its national self-confidence. And Mrs. Thatcher put that right."

Thatcher serves as a lesson in perseverance. She held to her ideals and in doing so opened Britain to become a more prosperous nation as well as one respected for its fortitude and resilience.[2]

*****

Margaret Thatcher had the skills to succeed as a politician and prime minister but perhaps her greatest attribute was her personal determination. It is one of our X factors, attributes that are essential to your ability to take charge of your life as well as to radiate the authority you need to bring others together for common purpose.

X factors are integral to leadership because they provide the backbone a leader needs to stand up and be counted, as well as the ability to do so with grace and dignity. Leaders are always on. The higher their profile, the bigger the stage; their words and actions are magnified by the outsize roles they hold. That is, a word from a CEO or commander rings with importance, but it also carries significance. Such leaders hold power over others, and therefore what they do is of consequence. Those in power who abuse their position lose the faith and trust of followers;

those who work hard at their jobs and try to do the right thing gain influence. People want to follow them because they trust them.

A case in point is provided by General John Allen when he served as the commander of NATO forces in Afghanistan from 2011 to 2013. He went to Afghanistan to begin the long process of handing military authority over to the Afghan forces that coalition troops were training. What he did not need were distractions, but, as every leader knows, heads of organizations rarely have the luxury of choosing issues. They must deal with the situation at hand, whatever comes their way. One crisis that Allen faced, which threatened to put the entire mission at risk, was the accidental burning of Korans at Bagram Airfield. Having spent much time in the Middle East, living in Muslim cultures, Allen knew that this situation was very serious. After all, this Koran burning came a year after the deliberate burning of a Koran by the provocateur Reverend Terry Jones in Florida, which was viewed by Muslims as an affront to their faith. Some, specifically the Taliban, would also seek to exploit the incident as an excuse for violence, and sadly it occurred.

As Allen explains: "So I believed that this could have conceivably been the end of the campaign. And so as I reached out across the entire command to grip the unfolding crisis that we were facing across all of Afghanistan, I was on two or three occasions every day speaking to all of my commanders, ensuring that they were calm on the process, engaging with their counterparts. We were in gun battles, not just with the Taliban, who was trying to leverage this crisis to their advantage to prove that we, 'the crusaders and the Jews,' as they called us, were in fact a cancer inside their society.

"So we were fighting the Taliban more intensively and we were now facing substantial and intense rioting around the country. And in doing that we successfully dealt with those crises across the entire country over a span of about six days. It was an unrelenting six days. It was six days of...moving from spot to spot trying to put out some really substantial potential crises where troops might have been in a gun battle or [where] we had casualties." Allen also got involved in recovering "the bodies of a couple of my officers who were killed in the Ministry of Interior."

How a leader invests himself and spends his time during a crisis is critical. As Allen explains, he was leading up—keeping his senior U.S. and NATO commanders, as well as the president, informed. He was also leading horizontally with President Hamid Karzai, "spending a great deal of time with President Karzai and his leadership to help him help himself and help him help me by keeping his rhetoric measured to keep this from flying out of control with the Afghan public."

Allen was also spending much time with his commanders. Moment to moment, Allen had to decide where his physical presence would be of the most value. As he says, that comes with experience as a commander. In addition to the application of fires and maneuver, the sustainment of the force, and critically, the commitment of the reserve, "one of the most important functions of a commander is how he or she uses their time and how he or she in the end maneuvers the presence of the commander to have the greatest possible moral effect at key points and times in the crisis."

Allen was not only engaged on the ground, he was linked via satellite to commanders back in the United States. As Allen explains, "My personal presence pervasively on the video teleconferences with my commanders a couple of times a day—and my personal presence at the moment of crisis around the country—went a long way toward keeping everybody calm and reacting to the crisis the way I wanted them to."

Few leaders will face the kind of mayhem that Allen did, but every leader will face crises that demand the best response possible. As Ryan Lance, CEO of ConocoPhillips, notes, "Strong leaders must be resilient." This is particularly true in the oil and gas business, which operates in a commodity market subject to wild swings in price and to boom-and-bust cycles. The business also requires a measure of guts to take its inherent risks. When it comes to exploration, "We only expect to succeed once in every three or four attempts we take to drill a conventional exploratory wildcat well."

Not only must leaders be resilient, they must project that spirit. Lance observes, "You have to trust the strategic direction you're pursuing and the objectives that you've set, because you'll always get a few curve balls that'll test your mettle and challenge the direction you're trying to take the company. You've got to keep your eye on the ball—being mindful of what the short-term environment is throwing at you, while also being consistent with the objectives you've laid out."

Leaders must provide clarity for people in the organization, freeing them from issues "they don't need to worry about, and instead letting the senior leaders worry about them," says Lance. "While the world is uncertain and changing around you, the leader must keep the team focused in the right direction. Attention shifts to specific tasks that are aligned with the goals we need to accomplish and milestones we need to reach. Those are the things that best motivate a team and keep them focused on the task at hand."

Such crises may run the gamut from a product recall, factory closing, or workplace fatality to day-to-day challenges that escalate. In those instances, leaders will need to call upon all the reserves they have—their X factors—not simply to survive but to hold their people and their organizations together under great adversity. Perseverance backed by determination does not come from thin air; it emerges from the character and convictions of those in charge.

It is essential to consider factors in addition to self-awareness that help personal growth. According to the 2013 *Time* Creativity Poll, those surveyed rated the following as the characteristics they most valued in others:

- 94 percent identified creativity
- 93 percent rated intelligence
- 92 percent said compassion
- 89 percent said humor
- 88 percent said ambition

Let's explore these attributes one by one.

Creativity

According to the *Time* survey, 71 percent of respondents said that both nature and nurture were factors in fostering creativity. Fifty-eight percent said it emerged from sudden inspiration while 32 percent thought that it occurred over time. Fifty percent of those surveyed said creative thoughts came to them in the form of pictures, while 34 percent formed their ideas in words.

Thirty-five percent of those surveyed said that the United States was the leader in creativity, compared with 23 percent who said China was the leader and only 19 percent who named Japan. For those who believed that America was not the leader—a majority of those surveyed—31 percent attributed the problem to schools, 30 percent to government, and only 17 percent to business. In fact, 55 percent of respondents said that technology is helping Americans be more creative versus 32 percent who said technology was hindering it. Bottom line, 62 percent of those surveyed said that "Creativity is more important to success in the workplace than they anticipated it would be when they were in school."[3]

Clearly, creativity is valued, and if organizations do not do enough, then it is up to individuals to develop it in themselves.

Intelligence

No leader can achieve much if he is lacking smarts. Intelligence is the raw horsepower needed to process information and make sense of it. And while processing power is highest in young people, the ability to apply it—knowledge—comes with experience. Intelligence is the baseline for competence. If an individual lacks the mental horsepower to do the job, then she will have little chance of succeeding.

It would be a mistake, however, to restrict intelligence to verbal and mathematical abilities alone. Harvard professor, psychologist, and best-selling author Howard Gardner has championed the cause of multiple intelligences. The multiple dimensions include spatial and kinetic, necessary for athletes; rhythmic, necessary for musicians; and interpersonal, vital for forming relationships, among others. Gardner has even made a case for existential or moral intelligence. The definition of morality is up to the individual; it may be put into practice through religious belief and practice, or it could be another form of mindfulness.[4]

Implementation of one's own capacity for multiple intelligences is essential to a leader's ability to lead. The awareness that you have the capacity to employ more than cognition to your leadership broadens your ability to think creatively, solve problems, and connect with others.

Compassion

Leadership literature is full of articles, even books, on the power of passion. While passion is essential to success at work—you need to love what you do—compassion is the element, as the *Time* survey shows, that others value. People want to know that their leaders care.

Compassion is a virtue rooted in the dignity of the individual. When you extend concern and offer care, you are saying that the person is worth it, and you want to do something to help. And it's the small things that matter.

Compassion takes many forms. We see it when employees pitch in to help a colleague in need. Sometimes the aid takes the form of a donation for a medical expense or hardship. Other times we see coworkers offer a fellow employee assistance by cleaning his house or shopping for groceries. And very often if an employee is out, her coworkers will band together to cover for the individual to make certain the work is done on time.

Humor

Life is hard and work is tough. Truisms, yes, but no less relevant in our daily lives! So when people can find laughter, it is something to be valued. Humor adds richness to our daily lives. Those who can look at a situation—whether at work, at home, or at play—and find humor are those we like to be around.

Every spring, a group of my friends (who all hail from Michigan) take a trip south to play golf. None of us excels at the game in the truest sense, and what brings us together is not the game but rather the camaraderie. Laughter is the stimulus that nurtures that camaraderie. We take pleasure in joshing one another and we roll in laughter like fifteen-year-olds at stupid jokes that one or another of us says. What I remember from these trips is not the golf courses or the accommodations or even the food, which are all good. I remember the spirit of levity that we share when we are together.

Having a sense of humor is a good attribute for a leader to possess. This is especially true when the leader turns the humor on himself. A leader who can laugh at his mistakes and poke fun at himself is one who is confident in his abilities and at the same time projects a sense of humanity and fun that draws people to him.

Humor is the great lubricant. It is a way to facilitate conversation and put people at ease. A master of this technique was Franklin Roosevelt, who projected a sunny persona; it complemented his sense of optimism. He also delighted in puncturing the egos of people in power, those who thought themselves better than the rest of us. Although a patrician by birth, Roosevelt as president knew how to speak to the common man, and at times his humor made him seem one of us. That was a secret to his ability to connect well with the American public.

Beware, however, of turning humor on others. Put-down humor can erode another's self-confidence, especially if the jokester is the boss. That has a debilitating effect on the subordinate's belief in himself. Others, too, pick up on the theme and look less favorably on the individual, even pitying him. That's deadly.

Ambition

While the *Time* survey ranked ambition a bit lower than other attributes (88 percent, compared with other attributes rated over 90 percent), one factor in its lower ranking may be that this survey measured attributes valued in others. Some of us may not like ambition in others, because we perceive highly ambitious people as overbearing or obnoxious. And while ambitious people can grate on us at times, ambition is an essential component in personal drive. Ambition sparks our internal motivators, it fuels our get-up-and-go, and it prompts us to tackle the challenges of the day.

Women in executive positions often face a backlash on the ambition dimension. There's a game I sometimes use in teaching in which I ask the group to describe a male executive who is hard-charging and aggressive. Such a person is often described as aggressive, but in a good way. A female executive, by contrast, might be described as "hell on wheels," and that's not a compliment.

Ambitious women need to project a softer edge while ambitious men can get away with being career driven. It is not fair, and it results in too many women hiding their abilities so they will not appear "too ambitious." Sadly, we need leaders who are bold as well as assertive. Ambition focuses energy on career goals, but it also provides a stimulus for action and execution.

Curiosity

While curiosity was not mentioned in the *Time* survey, many leaders value it and look for it in others. According to Ryan Lance, a curious leader is one who is trying to figure out why things are what they are. Jim Haudan, CEO of Root, says curiosity "is an insatiable desire to understand and to ask and to pursue and to question and to answer. Show me somebody who's curious and a lifelong learner and I'll show you somebody we can train in any way necessary to be successful in our business."

A curious leader is forever asking questions. She does this as a means of discovery, of provoking thought. A curious leader is one who is looking to find possibilities where others may have overlooked them. As Haudan notes, humility complements curiosity. A humble leader admits she does not have all the answers and is patient when explaining things to others, especially those who may not understand the concept the first time. Haudan says, "A humble leader meets people where they are at the moment. Not where he or she expects or wants them to be. [These leaders] actively try to understand what it is like 'not to know' so they can translate the complex language of strategy into a common language of shared meaning."

Curiosity is a powerful catalyst for leaders seeking to make positive change. Questions serve as ignition for exploration. A curious leader does not expect a single answer but rather an exploration of possibilities that can lead to new discoveries as well as new solutions.

Character

As important as the preceding attributes are, none is more important than character. It is the foundation upon which an individual and, certainly, leaders stand. Without it an individual lacks backbone. One of the best definitions of character I have encountered comes from Jeff Nelson, who established the OneGoal program in Chicago, which focuses on helping young people from disadvantaged backgrounds succeed in high school and later in college. The elements of character, as Nelson sees it, emerge from five aspects: integrity, resilience, resourcefulness, professionalism, and the one we just discussed—ambition.

For a column in Forbes.com, I put these attributes in the form of questions that leaders need to ask themselves. Here they are.[5]

1. *How do I manifest integrity?* Do I pay lip service, or do I live it even when it means making a sacrifice?
2. *How do I demonstrate resilience?* When our team faces an obstacle, what example do I set for them?
3. *How resourceful can I be?* When we are faced with limited resources, what do I do to help my team make the best of the circumstances?
4. *Do I act my role as a true professional?* Do I keep myself educated in my field, stay up-to-date on trends, and act on behalf of my team?
5. *Is my ambition working for me or against me?* That is, does my quest for success inhibit my ability to work well with colleagues and to collaborate with them?

Such questions provoke thoughts about the character we exhibit to others. After all, leadership, as is often noted, is about perception—how our followers perceive us. Leaders also invest themselves and their hopes in the character of others. Chester Elton tells a story about his former boss, Kent Murdock, who was the CEO of O.C. Tanner, where Elton worked for nearly two decades. As Elton puts it, Murdock was always great about saying, " 'Place your bet on character.' And so when Adrian [Gostick] and I were writing these books and we'd come up to different obstacles or tough things he'd always pull us aside and say, 'Don't worry about perception and what people are saying. I've bet on your character, and you're both of high character. You'll figure it out.' " It was brilliant, says Elton. "Kent challenged us to solve the problems but basically what he was saying was you've got my support. We never wanted to let him down. We knew he believed in us. And in turn we believed in him."

Fernando Aguirre, who served as CEO of Chiquita Brands, spent the first part of his career at Procter & Gamble (P&G).

He credits P&G with teaching him how to hire for character. "We all can teach and train and learn functional skills. But I think having the right character, having the right attitude in your DNA, is even more important than skills." With younger people, identifying character comes from looking at their experience at school as well as in other activities such as sports, the arts, or the community.

When hiring executives, Aguirre says he learned to discern character by listening to candidates talk about their job experiences. If they speak negatively of previous employers and supervisors, it's a warning sign that the individual is not a team player. He says, "You can ask enough questions to draw people out like that. I typically interview people for an hour and if I liked them I'd stay an hour and a half or two…" Later, he'd take them to lunch or dinner. "I would see their habits…and how they conducted themselves," Aguirre says. Not everyone made it to mealtime. As he notes, "I had interviews where, after twenty-five minutes, I said, 'All right. Thanks for coming.' And my assistant would know right away that this candidate was not getting hired."

Character becomes the person, but it does not exist in a vacuum. We see it manifest in attributes that support it. Consider the next few attributes.

Resilience

There is no shame in getting knocked down. It is what you do next that matters most. One man who knows what it is like to be pushed to the limits is General John Allen, a veteran of multiple combat tours. Here's how he describes a moment of truth he experienced in Iraq at the outset of what became known as the Anbar Awakening.

I remember on one particular occasion we had a really bad day in and around Fallujah, and I got back to my command post and sat down. The temperature was just scorching hot. And I sat down on the steps in front of the space [individual living quarters] in which I lived. It was an old beat-up Iraqi command post. It was now our command post. It was pretty good living, actually, by marine standards, but it wasn't much to look at. So I sat down on the steps outside of this building and we were exhausted and the temperature was blistering hot and, of course, we were still in Humvees at the time, we weren't yet in the MRAPS [Mine-Resistant Ambush Protected vehicles], which were much more protected.

The temperature in Humvees could get up to 135 or 140 degrees pretty easily. We had a really bad day and we'd taken a lot of casualties across Al Anbar, and I remember sitting there on the steps with my head in my hands and my helmet was off to my side. I think it was on my right-hand side. It was upside down so it was laying on its top and my M4 carbine, my rifle, was across my helmet. And I'm sitting there thinking my God, I'm a general officer in what's appearing to become a lost cause. I'm gonna be part of losing a war. And then suddenly I looked—I opened my eyes and I looked down and blood was just flowing from my nose. The whole business, the temperature, the environment, the pressure was such that the capillaries in my nose had opened up and there was this puddle of blood down between my feet. I thought to myself, I can't let this be the moment where I decide to give up. This has got to be one of those moments, a point in history, where I decide I've got to reach down inside me and turn this around.

Allen persisted. He carried out his mission and, as a result of efforts like his and that of thousands of other marines and army soldiers, the tide of war turned in 2007, in what became known as the Anbar Awakening. Anbar was supported by "the surge," an effort that allowed a measure of peace in Iraq and the eventual withdrawal of coalition forces from Iraq.

Courage

Many leaders have noted that courage is not the absence of fear, but rather the management of it. John Kennedy, who severely injured his back and lost his boat in the South Pacific in World War II, believed that courage was something to be endured. "The courage of life," wrote Kennedy, "is often a less dramatic spectacle than the courage of a final moment; but it is no less a magnificent mixture of triumph and tragedy. A man does what he must—in spite of personal consequences, in spite of obstacles and dangers and pressures—and that is the basis of all morality."

To my way of thinking, Kennedy's definition is closer to the reality that many of us face—outside of harm's way. Courage for us means choosing a moral path: putting what's right ahead of what's expedient. In that regard, we make choices to stand by our convictions and in the process make sacrifices that may initially hurt us, but in the long run instill character. True leaders also exert courage in service of others. They put themselves on the line in order to advance the career of a subordinate or even save the jobs of others by sacrificing part of their compensation so that one, two, or even more can hold their jobs in tough economic times. Courage comes in many forms and is integral to the ability to lead others.

Confidence

All of the factors we've discussed thus far are essential to individual development, but there is one additional X factor that is essential to bringing all of these attributes to bear in constructive ways. It is confidence. A leader without confidence is like a boat without a rudder, drifting aimlessly. There are many ways to think of confidence, but I like to think of it as the internal spirit of "can do." It emerges from within us all.

Confidence emerges from our accomplishments. It arises from what we have done and what we have learned, so that when we face the next challenge we have a reservoir of something inside of us that says, "Yes, I can do this." Consider confidence as a muscle. When you are first starting your career, that muscle may be underdeveloped. But with everything you accomplish, that muscle gets a little bit stronger; it even gets stronger with endeavors that do not go so well.

As much as confidence is internal, it has two external applications. When you are confident in yourself, others sense it, and, when coupled with what you have done well, they come to believe in it. Their sense of confidence in you reflects positively on you and adds to your confidence in yourself.

There is a third aspect to confidence, and that comes when you are able to instill it in others. I recall something that Kenneth Duberstein, who once served as chief of staff to President Ronald Reagan, said about the former president. He asserted that one of Reagan's gifts as a politician was the ability to get people to believe in themselves and their own abilities. When people believe in themselves anything is possible.[6]

Such insight is fundamental to sports coaching. So often a coach's true job, aside from drawing up plays and getting players to buy into the plan, is getting his team to buy into their collective abilities. That is, if they play together, they will have success. Confidence is an imperative, but individual players must believe in themselves before they can believe in the team.

Of course, there is such a thing as misplaced confidence. Someone who is unaware of how she is perceived by others may fall prey to overconfidence. This individual may not read the signals that others send. Think of Michael Scott in the television comedy *The Office*. Scott (as played by Steve Carell), is supremely confident in his abilities, but he is so self-absorbed and ill attuned to the feelings of others that he cannot see that they think he's a buffoon. Such individuals can become overconfident and even arrogant because they don't see themselves as others do.

Beware of False Gods

As we learned in chapter 1, mindfulness requires practice, but it also requires humility. In this regard, we can look to history for examples of leaders who failed to keep their egos in check. One egregious example was Alexander the Great. After conquering much of what was called the "known world," Alexander began to think of himself as a god. (In fairness, deities in Greek and Roman times were plentiful, so the line between mortality and immortality—at least in one's imagination—was not a broad leap, especially for heroic figures.)

Nonetheless, as Quintus Curtius Rufus, a Roman historian, notes in his *History of Alexander*, the conqueror began acting out, "punishing" those whom he distrusted. As Curtius notes, "Success can change one's own nature and rarely is anyone cautious enough to respect his own good fortune." While in Persia,

Alexander began expecting subordinates to prostrate themselves before him, a Persian tradition. Later, his army in India rebelled, refusing to go any further. They wanted to go home. There were death plots against him. He died in Babylon, possibly poisoned, though that account is in dispute.

What is not disputed is that Alexander's ego, like that of many leaders who end up meeting untimely ends, cost him the loyalty of many of his followers. It also damaged his legacy. Little of what he had gained was sustainable by his heirs, and his empire dissipated.[7]

It takes real effort for a successful leader to keep himself humble. Humility arises from perspective, and part of that perspective arises from knowing one's own limitations. As Fernando Aguirre puts it, "I realized when I became a CEO that it took me a year or two to learn how to be a CEO, and it's amazing how you get to those levels. Later on in life you realize that maybe you weren't as prepared and ready as you probably could have been. A very important aspect of this is you become more aware about the influence you have on others." Aguirre notes that CEOs of public companies are under tight scrutiny, especially in the era of social media, where behaviors good and bad can go public. Senior leaders are also subject to criticism. "Some people are constructive critics, many people are not," says Aguirre. "You just have to be aware that whatever you say and do could sometimes work against you. So it is a very important aspect of being a leader, in my opinion. You have to be mindful of yourself and you also have to be mindful of others because you may be impacting other people without knowing about it."

For one thing, some leaders lack what all good leaders must project: a sense of humility. Humility is a virtue, but in our hypercompetitive world it is something that gets shunted aside. Humility to the uninitiated is a sign of weakness. Just the opposite is true. Humility is a sign of strength. Think of it this way:

being confident enough to admit your shortcomings or mistakes does not make you a weakling; it demonstrates that you possess a degree of self-awareness.

Closing Thought: X Factor

The X factors delineated in this chapter are intended as thought starters. As important as they are, you can find other factors that contribute to success, yours and others'. The challenge for you is to find these factors and incorporate them into your leadership persona. Then you can lead in ways that bring people to you, so that together you can achieve intended results.

The sum of your X factor attributes gives you the foundation to do what you do better than anyone else. Your X factor could include a talent, that is, a proclivity for doing something well. Or it could be a skill, like a facility for working with data. Understanding your X factors is essential to your development.

Your X factor attributes are what people will come to know you for and rely upon you for. For example, if you are the kind of person who can get people focused and on task, that will make your reputation. Likewise, you may be a creative type, one who thinks of ideas to make things better.

Find ways to hone your X factor attributes. Look for opportunities to get better at what you do. This may come through on-the-job practice or through further training. You may also need to acquire more skills through additional schooling. Another way to improve your X factor attributes is by taking on new responsibilities. You can do this by becoming a team or project leader. Undertaking such a role will challenge you to expand your skill set, especially as it applies to connecting with others (as we will see in chapter 4).

The sum of a leader's accomplishments is how she has positively affected the organization. This is a leader's legacy, and it rests on a foundation of character, ambition, resilience, and perseverance.

X Factors = Right Stuff

Leadership Questions

- What are you doing to capitalize on your X factor attributes?
- What are you doing to apply the talent you have to the skills you possess?
- What can you do to ensure that you keep discovering new opportunities to grow and develop your talents and skills?

Leadership Directives

- Look for ways to focus on putting your character into action. Find ways to assert your inner convictions by setting an example that others want to follow.
- Find opportunities to apply your imagination. Are there tasks you could reduce or eliminate in favor of doing something more efficiently?
- Look for examples of compassion in your community. How are people you respect demonstrating a commitment to others in order to make a positive difference?

- Lighten up. Hard work is, well, hard, but that does not mean you cannot find some humor to ease the situation.
- Ambition fuels your drive. What are you doing to put your ambition into gear? Are you ambitious for the right reasons?
- Confidence is a feeling you get when you reflect on your accomplishments. How are you demonstrating it in the workplace?
- Develop your own X factor list. What is important to you and why?

4

Innovation

Investment decisions or personal decisions don't wait for the picture to be clarified.

ANDY GROVE

Make Change Work for You

Ryan Lance, CEO of ConocoPhillips, believes that people need to think beyond what they think is initially possible. "I tell people that human nature is not very amenable to change, so most people like the standard way of doing things. But I say that change equates to opportunity. If you look for opportunity to come out of change, you can always find it. You can spend your time looking for the difficult elements of change, but opportunities are always there. In our business there's another tenet that's important, and it's follow the capital or follow the growth. You want to go where the business is booming, where the growth is, where the capital is."

Change is something that Lance has embraced throughout his career. "As I reflect back on my own experience, some of the best career moves were made in the face of change. Specifically, I worked on integrating several mergers about a decade ago. This wasn't glamorous work, but it put me in a position to be on the frontline when we were merging Conoco and Phillips to create ConocoPhillips."

If you don't take a chance, you won't make a difference. That's a mantra that has served Lance well. "This job provided a unique opportunity for me to meet people on both sides of the company, because I had come from a third company as part of that merger. I got to see how each company operated, how they ran their businesses, and how they made tough allocation decisions around capital, people, and resources. I learned a lot about the functions that support the main business of engineering and operations, such as finance, legal, and human resources. I gained exposure to all facets of the business as I went through this. Again, at the time it didn't feel like a glamorous assignment, but I put myself in a position very purposefully to gain insights about the businesses and the different company cultures. Ultimately, I was better prepared to succeed in the new merged company as we moved forward."

Make the Most of a Challenge

Fernando Aguirre, former CEO of Chiquita Brands, was a rising executive at Procter & Gamble when he was given the opportunity to go to Brazil to see if he could turn around its failing operations. After Aguirre presented his three-year turnaround plan, the CEO of P&G, Edwin Artzt, said, "Fernando that's great, but three years is unacceptable. I want you to do it in one year." Aguirre had his doubts. "But I didn't tell anybody else that. I was then young and naïve and resilient. And I said [to myself], 'All right. I'll figure out a way.'"

Artzt also gave Aguirre permission to call him if he needed help. He told Aguirre: "You have a direct line to me anytime you need or want a decision that you don't get from anyone else." But Artzt did not give Aguirre a blank check; the turnaround needed to happen within a year, or P&G might close its operations in Brazil, and with it the careers of Aguirre and his Brazilian colleagues.

Not only was Aguirre on a short time frame, he had to find a way to make a newly built factory that produced Pampers diapers succeed. Its losses were dragging down the Brazilian operation. One reason was that the product line was too diverse—different Pampers for boys and girls, both in multiple sizes. Aguirre and his team slimmed the product line to unisex diapers in just three sizes—small, medium, and large. That move did the trick.

As Aguirre explains, "We broke even the first year. We made $8 million the second year. We made $25 million the third year and my fourth year we made $45 million of profitability and the revenue was $450 million. That made my career."

RESEARCH SAYS...
OF TOP 20 COMPANIES FOR LEADERSHIP,
RESPONDENTS SAY THAT:

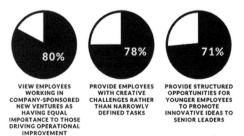

80%
VIEW EMPLOYEES WORKING IN COMPANY-SPONSORED NEW VENTURES AS HAVING EQUAL IMPORTANCE TO THOSE DRIVING OPERATIONAL IMPROVEMENT

78%
PROVIDE EMPLOYEES WITH CREATIVE CHALLENGES RATHER THAN NARROWLY DEFINED TASKS

71%
PROVIDE STRUCTURED OPPORTUNITIES FOR YOUNGER EMPLOYEES TO PROMOTE INNOVATIVE IDEAS TO SENIOR LEADERS

SOURCE: 2013 BEST COMPANIES FOR LEADERSHIP HAY GROUP[1]

Innovation. Individuals who have moxie are not content with the status quo. They are continually seeking to acquire new skills and apply them in new ways.

Sergio Marchionne

He does not look the part of an automotive mogul, with his sweater, cigarette, and slightly rumpled clothing. But looks in this case do not tell the story. He may be the auto executive with the most challenging job in the world: reviving the fortunes of two flagging automakers, Fiat and Chrysler. His name is Sergio Marchionne, and as CEO of both automakers, he led a turnaround effort that startled those who do not know him, though it has not surprised those familiar with his track record.

Marchionne was born in Italy but immigrated to Toronto with his family when he was a teenager. The fact that he did not speak English was a stumbling block, and his teen years in school were not marked by academic success. But unlike others his own age, he did have a remarkable ability at cards. He would accompany his father to the local Italian solidarity club and join in games of poker with his elders. His tolerance for risk was high and he seemed to keep his cool, two traits that would hold him in good stead in his career.

After buckling down to the books, he went to university and did well enough to earn a degree in chemistry. He gained a job with a Swiss company, and ended up in various manufacturing positions in Brazil and Europe. Marchionne proved himself an adept manager and ended up running SGS, a Swiss subsidiary of Fiat. He turned the company around, which earned him the notice of Fiat's senior management.

As the twenty-first century dawned, the company that had defined Italian manufacturing prowess—and was involved in many other businesses as well—was foundering. The biggest cash drain was Fiat Auto, and Marchionne was tapped to run it. Urgency was the order of the day, as the company was close to insolvency. Some executives would have withered under the assignment; Marchionne did just the opposite. He thrived.

Jennifer Clark, who profiled Marchionne in her book *Mondo Agnelli: Fiat, Chrysler, and the Power of a Dynasty,* writes, "Marchionne's unusual ability is that he can see what actually needs to be done, and then cajoles and goads his flat management structure of dozens of direct reports in weekend meetings to achieve the goal." A UBS analyst put it best: "Marchionne doesn't let go. That's what his strength is. He is good at strategy *and* at execution." Under Marchionne, both Fiat and Chrysler have turned the corner, at least for now.

The balance between vision and execution is akin to right- and left-brain thinking. A visionary thinks about what can happen; he envisions the future in very specific terms, not simply in outcomes but in what it will take to produce the outcomes. The execution part is getting people in place and providing them with resources to succeed. It also means holding people's feet to the fire.

Marchionne can be a demanding boss. He expects his top lieutenants to burn the midnight oil, including working weekends. The work is tough, but he holds himself to the same standards he expects from his team. When Marchionne took over Fiat and Chrysler, heads rolled. But with both companies in dire straits, decisive action was necessary. In times of crisis a leader must often move quickly. That said, Marchionne has a sense of humility. When he spoke to Chrysler employees for the first time, in 2009, he said that he needed their ideas and their effort to succeed.

Marchionne likes to be close to the action. At Fiat he spent time walking around getting to know people, and when he identified his key people he pulled them toward him in a matrix management style that enabled everyone to stay close. At Chrysler he did the same. As one executive commented, by working closely together, employees kept one another in alignment with corporate directives.

Marchionne did not take over the plush office on the top floor of Chrysler's headquarters. Instead, he located his office on the engineering floor, to be close to the people who were revamping the product line.

He insisted that the Fiat engineering team share its expertise with Chrysler engineering teams, a process that would accelerate the development of smaller vehicles to meet the automaker's need for improved fuel efficiency. He also empowered his managers to take a look at the Chrysler lineup, especially Jeep, an iconic brand.[2]

In making these changes, Marchionne sent a signal that he was actively engaged in the business, but that if the company was to be successful it would need to think and do differently. It would need to innovate, and in this regard, he is a model of a leader who exemplifies what it takes to energize an organization through the spirit of innovation.

*****

Good leaders are those who, by nature or by training, learn to look over the horizon. Like scouts, they are attentive to any form of change, such as a shift in consumer preferences, the rise of a new competitor, or the altered landscape of an economy. They are forever comparing what is happening now to what happened before and what could happen next. They are tuned to the future. Their forward-themed outlook is not merely one of observation, it is one of application. That means that, even as they assess what is happening now, they are thinking about what's next. That gives rise to innovation.

Creativity, which we explored in the previous chapter, is essential to innovation. It is up to managers to find ways to encourage it so that employees can use it. Innovation, to my way of thinking, is applied creativity. Leaders have to enable employees to be creative by providing conditions that let the imagination flourish. They also must take what emerges and push, or pull, it throughout the organization. And that is not easy.

Obstacles to Innovation

Many organizations regard innovation as the Holy Grail, that is something for which they are searching. It provides the path a company needs to become more creative, productive, and ultimately more profitable. According to one global study of major companies, senior executives rated the need for innovation as a nine or ten on a ten-point scale. They viewed innovation as a source of growth. Sounds good, but more and more there is pessimism about innovation. This same study showed that these executives rated their satisfaction with innovation at no better than five on a ten-point scale.[3]

Obstacles to innovation fall into three categories. One is hitting a plateau, not because there is less innovation but because the returns are smaller. For example, as described in *The Economist*, the biggest gains in life style comfort and productivity came from "electricity, internal combustion engines, plumbing, petrochemicals, and the telephone." These are all delivering good returns, but not quantum returns. Could there be new technologies in the future? Of course, but no one has yet identified what they are.[4]

Two, innovation contributes to productivity but, as economists Tyler Cowens and Charles Jones have shown, productivity has decreased. For example, according to research, "in 1950 the average R&D worker in America contributed almost seven times more to 'total factor productivity' "—return on investment, so to speak—than he did in the year 2000. Furthermore, it's taking longer to innovate because technology is racing to catch up to science.[5]

Three, innovation today seems slower than it once was. The improvements to household living—electricity, refrigeration, air conditioning—occurred in the previous century. Medicine has enabled humans to live much longer: life expectancy in the United States is over seventy-eight years. Yet the killer ailments—heart disease, cancer, stroke, and organ failure—remain with us, despite hundreds of billions of dollars spent on research.

The slowdown in innovation may hinder national productivity. The average growth rate of U.S. productivity in the twentieth century was 2 percent. Robert Gordon, an author and professor of social science at Northwestern University, argues that future growth may average 1 percent. Invention in the last quarter of the nineteenth century, as Gordon explains, fueled innovation starting with electricity, indoor plumbing, and the internal combustion engine. The post-World War II period saw the introduction of jet travel and the proliferation of computer processing, and in the last decade of the twentieth century "the marriage of communications to computer" spread the power of the Internet, which today rules nearly every aspect of business. Repeating such breakthroughs, as Gordon says, will be difficult.[6]

Obstacles to innovation will only increase, but that does not mean we should abandon our quest for it. We simply need to explore new ways of looking at it. That begins with leadership. It falls to leaders to create conditions in which individuals can contribute ideas about how to work more efficiently and productively. Such openness may not lead to breakthroughs, but over time they will spark patterns of behavior that encourage people to talk about issues and challenges and how to solve them. It is only within this milieu that creativity can occur, and in turn be applied to innovation.

Setting Ground Rules for Innovation

CEO Rich Sheridan's firm, Menlo Innovations, true to its name, makes its livelihood by innovating. A programmer from his teens, Sheridan believed that there had to be a better way to create software, which spurred him to create a company that did things differently. Sheridan said, "Where I learned to manage by mimicking other people above me was in environments of fear...And you're like, 'Oh, that's the way you manage people.'" It was fear. It was artificial fear.

"Managers would say to employees, 'Are you staying late this weekend? I mean, we got a deadline to meet. If we don't meet that deadline we're gonna lose that account. If we lose that account that could cost you your job.' And it's like, was any of that true? I have no idea, but I'm going to work this weekend. But now I'm operating out of fear. You're not going to get innovation in an environment like that."

Chester Elton agrees: "I think the biggest inhibitor to innovation in organizations that I've seen is where failure is punished. The message is, 'Boy, you better be sure that this is gonna work because if it doesn't work heads will roll.' Companies that are most innovative to me embrace failure."

So when Sheridan founded Menlo Innovations with his business partner in 2001, he resolved, "Number one thing, hands down, you have to pump fear out of the room. You cannot innovate in an environment of fear because fear causes your body to produce the powerful chemicals adrenaline and cortisol. These chemicals shut down the most interesting parts of your brain, because the blood is now being channeled to your extremities so you can run and to your heart so you get enough oxygen to run. Blood is channeled away from the front—prefrontal cortex of the brain. And now you've lost all ability to be creative, to be imaginative, to be innovative, because now you're in reptile mode.

"So creating the right environment and working hard to get fear out of the room is important. If people aren't afraid they will begin to trust one another. If they trust one another they might begin to collaborate. And if they collaborate suddenly you will get creativity, innovation, imagination! And that's what companies are looking for."

Driving out fear is only the first step; you need to take it further, according to Sheridan. "We want joy here, defined as the people for whom we're designing and building the software love what we've done. They are delighted and we've made their lives better. So that's that whole idea of working on something bigger than yourself.

"We focus our cultural intention on the outside world, on the effect we're going to have on the world. And I think that's really important. And all of our processes, all of our behaviors, all of our hiring practices, everything we do is built out of a shared belief system that all of us in the room believe will produce that kind of joyful outcome for our customers. And so I think intentional culture and the shared belief system that brings that intentional culture to life every day is what makes all the difference."

Discipline of Innovation

Innovation does not occur by accident. It requires discipline. Ryan Lance, CEO of ConocoPhillips, says, "Leaders must be patient and willing to tolerate mistakes and failures. Like we say in our business, 'You've got to be willing to drill a few dry holes.' So innovation is not a quick thing; it takes time. I think you have to set the right tone culturally. You have to let people know it's okay to ask and it's okay to dream."

"Innovation for the sake of innovation may be noble," says Lance, "but to be practical, it has to be capable of being transported to the field; it has to have a business application; and it has to impact the business in a visible way. You also need to understand the economics of innovation. At the end of the day we have to be good stewards of shareholder money, and as leaders we have to show that innovation will improve upon the business."

The willingness to move swiftly is an imperative when it comes to innovation. As Aguirre says, "I think most people now realize that if you're not changing and evolving your business models you're not going to be successful." Once managers were told to hold to strategies for a decade. "You can't do that anymore," says Aguirre. "The world is so fast. The world is changing so much. Competition is better. Technology is now so advanced that everyone is developing products as good as or better than yours. So you have to keep improving, and there's no way to improve your business models, whether you make or sell products, or whether you are in the service industry, you can't improve without some level of innovation."

Aguirre emphasizes the need to support innovation: "You need to put effort and investment behind it. At Chiquita we ended up investing a ton of money my first five years to expand the brand. The brand is fantastic, very powerful, very well known, but we only had it in bananas. And I felt that one of the most important things we needed to do was diversify the company into other product categories and also to expand the brand. We needed to leverage a fantastic brand. So we invested and I talked a lot about the expansion and diversification of the business."

Innovate in New Ways

"The key to being consistently innovative," argue Drew Boyd and Jacob Goldenberg, authors of *Inside the Box: A Proven System of Creativity for Breakthrough Results*, "is to create a new form for something familiar and then find a function it can perform." The authors cite the example of a contact lens; it's a corrective lens without a frame. This is a form of subtraction. Addition would be adding lenses together, such as telephoto or close-up lenses. Nestlé did something similar when it developed a line of iced teas to be drunk warm or heated during colder months. The beauty of this approach, argue professors Boyd and Goldenberg, is that "The most consequential ideas are often right under our noses, connected in some way to our current reality or view of the world."[7]

Ways to innovate are as myriad as business models. In fact, one form of innovation has no real business model at all. We call it "Big Science," a collaborative effort among many different interests to build one thing. An example is ATLAS, the world's largest microscope. As described in *The Economist*, ATLAS is "45 meters long, 25 meters tall, and weighing as much as the

Eiffel Tower." ATLAS resides in a cavern, where it is used by scientists at CERN "to probe the fundamental building blocks of matter."

The secret to ATLAS's success is the buy-in that thousands of engineers and scientists from around the world have devoted to it. Their motive was not profit, it was exploration. And for that reason it has been a success. Physicists using it proved the existence of the Higgs boson, known as the "God particle" because it may be a part of everything we know, large or small. What the nonscientific world can learn from Big Science is that innovation can occur on a global scale if people are united in purpose.[8]

One company with ambitions like those of Big Science is Google. And with a research and development budget approaching $7 billion (as of 2013), it has the heft as well as the brain power to make it happen. Google's biggest asset, however, may be the commitment of its cofounder Sergey Brin. While Larry Page serves as CEO, Brin is the chief technology officer. He has direct involvement in Google's laboratory, Google X, which is inspired by such past labs as AT&T's Bell Labs and Xerox's PARC.

"Sergey's direct involvement," says Richard DeVaul, who works at Google X as a rapid evaluator, "is one of the ways this environment gets supported." Such personal commitment, according to *Bloomberg Businessweek*'s Brad Stone, who wrote about Google X, is one reason that the lab is able to attract top-notch talent.

Key projects include Google Glass, a computer in eyeglasses form, and the self-driving automobile, both favorites of Brin himself. But the lab is more ambitious. Its head, Eric "Astro" Teller, addressed the 2013 South by Southwest (SXSW) conference by saying, "The world is not limited by IQ. We are all limited by bravery and creativity." On the drawing board are

projects like an airborne turbine that generates power by flying in circles, as well as an initiative to bring Internet access
to undeveloped parts of the world. Their mission is bold—
moonshots for technology and science. As Stone wrote, Google
X (the Google innovation laboratory) is designed to make "those
million-to-one scientific bets that require generous amounts
of capital, massive leaps of faith, and a willingness to break
things."[9]

Google also sponsors the Solve for X project, which hosts
conventions centered around a collaborative approach to solving
global issues; one conference included presentations on inflat-
able robots, detection of early Alzheimer's via eye exams, and
nuclear fusion reactors. As Teller puts it, "We're as serious as a
heart attack at making the world a better place."

That statement sums up what is necessary for innovation. Funding yes, but also the faith to experiment as well as
the recognition that failure is an option. While line managers
often do not have access to the spigot that controls the flow of
capital, they can encourage their people to think for themselves
and to undertake new projects with the understanding that
mistakes will occur—and when they do, they can serve as vital
lessons.

Innovation: Systems Approach

What works for Rich Sheridan at Menlo Innovations is a systems approach to innovation: "We pair our [software program-
mers] together, two to a computer for five working days, and
then we switch the pairs every five days. It ensures that everybody on the team is going to interact with everybody else on the
team."

The office has an open-space setup. Sheridan said: "We're all working in the same room together, with no walls, offices, cubes, or doors. This means that at least we're spending time together." Such proximity fosters conversation and coordination that create opportunities for people to collaborate with one another to get the work done. Project tracking is precise but somewhat old-fashioned, especially for a technology firm. "We've created an interesting system of no ambiguity where we write stuff down on these little story cards," said Sheridan. "We pin the story cards on the wall under people's names. So people come in and they know exactly what they should be working on. And now they can actually get meaningful things done."

The systems approach welcomes client interaction. "In our world, we invite our clients in every five business days," said Sheridan. "And they reconnect with us in an event we call a 'show and tell.' And our 'show and tell' is actually reverse 'show and tell.'" Rather than Menlo staffers revealing the work to date, the clients present it to the programmers. "By pulling our client into the process that way, they're now mindful of the work we've just done...Software is very theoretical until it's actually working, until people can actually touch it."

It is important for staffers to see the clients interact with the software. As Sheridan says, "The clients are the ones with their hands on the keyboard touching the software," with the people who worked on that software watching. There is "no interpretive dance in between, no ambiguity, see the emotion, see the eyebrows, see the folded arms, see the delight, see the smiles, hear the laughter, see the frowns, all that kind of stuff I think is really important."

These client sessions also head off potential problems. "I mean, the fact that we get good feedback is great. It's far more

important when we get the negative feedback, hopefully constructive negative feedback. And one of the ways we make it
constructive is we're doing these check-ins every five business
days, so if we made mistakes they're not going to be big ones.
They're going to be little ones."

"Think in Glass"

You don't have to be a twenty-first-century company to innovate. In Murano, the glass-blowing district of Venice, innovation continues to be a watchword. And it has to be. According
to the *The Economist*, contemporary glassworks, often located
in Asia, are undermining this seven-hundred-year-old Venetian tradition. More than a third of glassmakers have shut their
doors, and many continue to ply their trade by making kitschy,
heavy glass souvenirs tourists once bought by the boatload. But
that way of glassmaking is not the future.

Adriano Berengo, a glassmaker, continues to operate his
Murano studio, but he has divided it into two parts. One side
produces traditional glass; the other side he offers to artists.
"Artists love new toys to work with," Berengo said. "What we
have to do is get them to think in glass." Artists working in
Berengo's studio produce two works of art—one for the studio
and the second for themselves, which they can put up for sale
themselves. If a third piece is produced, Berengo and the artist
split the take.

Murano, as *The Economist* noted, has prospered "through
innovation, and concentrating on quality." With innovators
like Berengo and others, Murano may be able to add another
century of tradition to its legacy. Again, innovation is not
New Age; it belongs to any age. Nowhere is this more so than

in Murano. Researching Venetian glass archives, Berengo discovered a way to make green glass using a technique from the sixteenth century called *avventurina*. Sometimes innovation involves looking backward to find ideas that may have been forgotten, but which have new applications in today's world.[10]

Ask Questions and Listen

General John Allen, as the senior-most commander in Afghanistan, used to hold regular sessions with his senior staff, including three-star generals from Britain and France and three- and two-star combat commanders. He would present them with a big question, such as, "How do we get after corruption in Afghanistan?" or "When and how do we begin to turn over military/operational lead to Afghan forces?" (This latter question raises an agenda that General Allen is credited with turning into a success, as he was the commander who initiated the turnover in 2011.)

"The idea was to draw out my commanders," Allen said. "You wouldn't find more experienced combat leadership probably anywhere on the planet in one small spot—to bring them all together to create a common perspective and mentality on issues where we could have a good, strong give-and-take." There was also push back. "If I felt that push back was valuable ultimately to me, providing greater focus or clarity in my orders or to change the order because it now makes better sense because of what I've heard, I've never hesitated to do that." A leader's job is to listen to what her direct reports say. "I think that's a healthy environment to have. If they believe that, no matter what they say to you, you won't change whatever it is you're doing, then that effect is, it ultimately chills the kinds of conversation that you want to have between leaders, especially leaders in combat," said Allen.

"Chalk the Field"

Jim Haudan, CEO of Root, says, "Innovation can only occur with the mind-sets that recognize that Big Ss come from small Fs, and that means big successes can only come from small failures. So if we can't fail we will never succeed." To do that, organizations must "fail forward fast," says Haudan. "You need to hug the failures and embrace the failures" rather than run from them.

Chester Elton concurs: "One other thing I've found about innovative companies is when they go down the track of something that's not working, they fail fast. So they figure out what it is, they take a shot at it, if it's not working they kill it quick and they move on. So I think innovative thinkers and organizations are those that take measured chances, but they don't let failure get in their way and they don't punish failure."

Toward that end, Haudan advises leaders to limit risk and go for "small, fast, and cheap." For example, go for process improvements and incremental changes to products rather than entire new product lines. Use them as learning lessons rather than "bet-the-company options." Once you have learned, you can take bigger risks, developing entirely new products or even product categories. Lessons learned on small bets will put the organization in a better position to take advantage of new opportunities.

Haudan notes a pitfall of innovation: applying it where it is not needed. "Innovation requires different management than operations," he says. So he advocates that you "chalk the fields," that is, determine what you will change and why. "There are places where you want absolutely no innovation, because reliability and predictability are key," says Haudan. For example, security in bank or patient safety must be fail-safe operations. These are areas where you don't take chances.

Reinventing Old Things

Innovation need not always be about what's new. Ryan Lance, CEO of ConocoPhillips, says, "[Innovation] can be coming up with new ways to do old things. That includes getting rid of old work processes that don't really add value to the company, its direction, culture, or the strategic objectives we're trying to fulfill." Innovation also requires "thinking about new ways to do existing processes while also killing old processes that don't make any sense."

Finding new ways of tackling old problems reinforces a culture of innovation. "If you pick the right opportunity, you can get a lot of mileage out of telling success stories. The stories go viral within the company and people recognize that, 'Hey, we did something different,'" says Lance. Employees will note the change and say to themselves, "They killed this inefficient process. I don't have to do this anymore. Isn't that a great thing?" When such changes are publicized, notes Lance, "You get a lot of visibility and credibility for your willingness to innovate."

Whether you find new applications for new technologies or use old ideas that offer new solutions, innovation is essential to the health of the enterprise. It falls to the leader to continue to push the organization to embrace creative ideas as a means of thinking and doing differently.

Closing Thought: Innovation

Innovation is often a work in progress. Sometimes people are willing to embrace something new, and when they do they expect instant results. As with many things in life, you have to keep doing it to become successful. More often, people resist innovation because it disrupts their comfort zone. When it does, they put up resistance. Again, it is necessary to keep trying. It falls to the mindful leader—one who looks for opportunity—to push the organization to do something different in the quest for improvement.

Innovation = Creativity + Application

Leadership Questions

- What are you doing to capitalize on your creative self?
- What do you do when you find your creative skills are not wanted?
- How are you helping others to maximize their creative abilities?

Leadership Directives

- Complacency is the bedmate of the status quo. Seek change and consider how it applies to you.

- Innovation is a change process. Apply your creative self to the situation around you. Sometimes you will innovate in your career, do something different. Other times you will need to innovate with your team to enable them to go in a new and different direction.
- Innovation begins with the openness to new ideas. Challenge yourself to embrace the possibility of change. And yes this will be disruptive.
- Learn to follow through on ideas that will improve things for your team, your customers, and your organization, not to mention yourself.
- Become a "go-to person" by using your creativity to effect positive change. You can do this by suggesting (or being open to) new ideas, solving problems, and collaborating with others.

5

Engagement

Let no one ever come to you without leaving better and happier.

MOTHER TERESA

A Better Way for People to Work Together

Rich Sheridan was looking to do something differently in software design. He had become frustrated by traditional methods, and in 1999 he read *Extreme Programming* by Kent Beck. He'd also seen a documentary on the process the design firm IDEO used to redesign a shopping cart on the ABC show *Nightline*. Once he became a vice president in an established company, he was in a position to implement his ideas: "And within six months I had transformed the R and D team, which affected the entire organization, and I got two years to run it and perfect it.

"Then in 2001 the Internet bubble burst and for the first time in my career I was out of work. The California company that had bought us shuttered every remote office they had, including our Ann Arbor operation. And now here I was having achieved my goal. I had this great organization. It was rocking and rolling and now it was all taken away from me. So that was the next level of adversity. I went home to my wife and I said, 'Honey, I got—lost my job today.' And she said, 'You're unemployed?' I said, 'No, I'm an entrepreneur now.'"

As Rich explains, he knew that what he had built for his previous company was a concept for software development that would be transferable to another company, one he would develop with his partner. "As my father would always say," notes Sheridan, "'Sometimes things that look like the worst turn out to be the best.'"

Introverts Know How to Engage Others

In 2006 Adam Grant, a management professor at the Wharton School, was a graduate student in organizational psychology. He was asked by his mentor, Brian Little, if he would be interested in meeting with Susan Cain, a lawyer-turned-author who was writing a book on the power of introverts. As Grant says, "[Cain and I] had what was supposed to be a thirty-minute meeting and it turned into about three hours. I was just totally fascinated by what she was studying. As I talked with her, I realized that there was a huge imbalance in research on introverts and extroverts, in that we had all this evidence that extroverts were more likely to be selected for leadership roles, that we look at extroverts and we tend to assume they're charismatic, they're gregarious, they're socially skilled, lots of things that are useful for leaders. Also, extroverts are much more attracted to leadership roles, because it's a situation where you experience a lot of stimulation, you get to be the center of attention, [and there are] lots of opportunities to be assertive.

"There are also studies showing that people rated extroverts as better leaders. But I couldn't find a single study, as Susan went through her list of questions for me, that actually linked extroverted leadership with better performance. And there was a moment where I think in a lot of cases I would have just said, 'Wow, that's a big gap, somebody ought to study that.'

"Susan got me so fired up. She was so eloquent and so curious and so thoughtful about this topic that I decided I was gonna start digging around to see if there was an opportunity to study that and never would have done it had Brian not put Susan on my radar."

RESEARCH SAYS...

OF TOP 20 COMPANIES FOR LEADERSHIP, RESPONDENTS SAY THAT:

85%	84%	82%
ACTIVELY MANAGE A POOL OF SUCCESSORS FOR MISSION-CRITICAL ROLES	OFFER LEADERSHIP DEVELOPMENT OPPORTUNITIES FOR EMPLOYEES	LEADERS WORK HARD TO CONNECT PEOPLE WITH PROJECTS THAT ARE PERSONALLY MEANINGFUL TO THEM

SOURCE: 2013 BEST COMPANIES FOR LEADERSHIP HAY GROUP[1]

Engagement. Persons with moxie seek to engage with the wider community around them. They are focused on making a positive difference in their teams and in their organizations.

Dolly Parton

The thing that resonates most with me about Dolly Parton is heart. You hear it in her songs and she acts on it in her life.

While some might be distracted by her over-the-top looks—big hair, big smile, and big bosom—it is her voice that attracts the most attention. It is at once soulful and playful. It radiates joy as well as sorrow. Most of all, it registers sincerity, and for that reason she has forged a relationship with her fans that spans generations.

Few would have predicted that a woman, one of twelve children, from humble origins in Sevierville, Tennessee, would rise to such prominence as a singer–songwriter, selling more than 100 million records. Her hardscrabble beginnings, coupled with her love of family, steeled her determination to pursue her craft. She was not only singing, but also writing songs as a youngster. Parton turned professional at age ten and appeared on local radio and television in Knoxville. As a young teen, she made her first appearance on country music's (then) biggest stage–the Grand Ole Opry. After graduating from high school, she moved to Nashville.

By age twenty-one she was appearing regularly on TV's *The Porter Wagoner Show,* singing duets with Wagoner. She had a string of country music hits and won the Country Music Award for female vocalist in 1975 and 1976. After that came more hits, but the wider appeal did not deter Parton from going back to her roots in gospel as well as bluegrass.

Essence of Dolly

To me, her song "Better Get to Livin' " offers insights that every leader ought to keep at the ready. That song, the lead track of her 2008 album *Backwoods Barbie*, allows Parton, the Oprah of Appalachia, to reveal the secret of her long career—"living, giving, forgiving, and some lovin'. " Not only do these words make good sense for country music enthusiasts, they make sense for leaders. Let's take them one at a time.

Living. Leaders need to be mindful of their situation and the situations of those they lead. They are aware of the impact their actions have on others and they seek to do what is best for the organization.

Giving. Leaders give of themselves so others can succeed. That means you spend time coaching and developing your people. Provide them with guidance to help them build upon their strengths, overcome their shortcomings, and give them a shoulder to cry on when times are tough.

Forgiving. People make mistakes. If they acknowledge it and seek to make amends, move forward. Get over it. A leader cannot afford grudges; it rubs off negatively on others and drains energy from the team.

Loving. Apply this to your work. Have a passion for what you do; it will inspire the entire team. A leader who enjoys her work and the people with whom she works is one who encourages people to follow her lead.

There are a few other words that Parton uses in this song that also apply to leadership behavior. Among them are *knowing*, understanding your values; *shining*, standing up for yourself; and *showing*, letting others know you care. And there is another word Parton uses—*healing*. Leaders must exert themselves to bring people together. Rifts need to be breached, wounds bound, and feelings assuaged. All of these are leadership responsibilities.

Success came early for Parton, but not without some hardship and sacrifice. All of her trials, tribulations, and joys are reflected in her music. Not only does she play and sing, she writes much of her own material. She has created a business enterprise worth hundreds of millions and yet is not without ironic humor about herself. She says, "It takes a lot of money to look this cheap." With her "glad to know ya" smile and country soprano voice, Dolly Parton knows her audience, and time and again she delivers what they want to hear. The woman knows her heart and herself.

Wider Appeal

Success in music led Parton to Hollywood. She made her film debut in the 1980 movie about savvy secretaries called *9 to 5*, for which she got an Academy Award nomination. Three decades later she penned music and lyrics for a musical version of *9 to 5* that played in Los Angeles and later on Broadway.

Her major entrepreneurial effort is Dollywood, a theme park, which opened in 1986 and is located in Pigeon Forge, Tennessee. Not surprisingly, Parton's financial advisors told her not to do the project. She told them, "Well, I'm gonna do it anyway, because I know it's the right thing to do in my gut." The park has thrived, and in 2013 she announced a ten-year $300 million expansion of the facility.

One interest that radiates from Parton's heart is her reading program. For the past two decades, Parton has been giving books to children as a means of fostering literacy. She founded

Imagination Library and, as she said on PBS's *NewsHour*, "Everywhere I go, the kids call me 'Book Lady.'" As Parton explains, "It really...started out as a very personal thing for me...originally meant for the folks in my home county...There were not books in our house growing up." Her father was illiterate, which Parton describes as a "crippling thing for him." Today, her Dollywood Foundation sends books to kids in 1,700 communities throughout the United States, Canada, and England.

"The older I get the more appreciative I seem to be of the book lady title," says Parton. "It makes me feel more like a legitimate person, not just a singer or entertainer. But it makes me feel like I have done something good with my life and with my success." You hear in those words the little girl born into poverty who rose above it with her talent, her commitment to her art, and her genuine engagement with others. In 2006 Parton was recognized by the Kennedy Center for her contribution to the arts, a rare tribute for a performer with country roots.

Dolly Parton's life as reflected through her art and in her actions is a shining example of what it means to live with heart. She reflects the essence of engagement, of putting yourself into your work. Leaders must foster commitment from others but first must be committed themselves. Dolly Parton shows us how that can happen.[2]

*****

Leaders do not work in isolation. They work with others in order to bring their ideas, their dreams, and their aspirations to fruition. To do this they must engage with others. The engagement can be as simple as one-on-one conversations that lead to relationships, or it can be engagement with groups, teams, or entire organizations. Engagement is an essential part of extending the leadership self in order to make a positive difference. It is also the ability to keep those who follow your lead focused on what it takes to turn goals into reality.

In this chapter my approach will be to tell the story of engagement from several perspectives. Here you'll encounter multiple models, from both the profit and nonprofit sectors. There is no one-size-fits-all approach to engagement, but there is a fundamental principle to which all highly engaged workplaces adhere. It is this: there is dignity in work, and when we treat workers with dignity they become contributors to results as well as to success.

Jim Haudan, CEO of Root, a visionary strategy and learning company, says his company "Is driven by the cause that people are not bringing the best version of themselves to the workplace. [We] want people to be engaged, but for some reason fear permeates the workplace." Strategy is important but what truly matters, according to Haudan, is "when people come together with aspirations to build something that doesn't exist." The challenge is to focus on purpose, or, as Haudan says, move from the "unconscious to the conscious. [This] invigorates the power of human beings to make a difference."

Doing this is Haudan's life's work. Originally an educator, he earned an MBA and then came to Root, where he combines his passion for teaching and learning with running a business. Now as CEO, his passion is "to get people off the bench and in the game of their work life so they can have two things: a sense of meaning and purpose from being part of something bigger than themselves, and [pride] in the results that can be achieved together" with other like-minded people. That is engagement in a nutshell.

Engaging with Purpose

The question is, how do we engage with purpose? First, leaders must enable others to recognize purpose on two levels—organizationally and personally. Leaders must instill purpose by linking what a company does (its mission) to what it wants to become (its vision). They do this through their communications and their actions. They leverage purpose as the why of work, that is, why do we do what we do? Then, as Haudan explains, it is up to leaders to give people a chance to buy in. In a recent workshop Haudan conducted with Robert Quinn, a professor of organizational development at the University of Michigan, attendees had the opportunity to link their personal stories to the story of their organization. It resonated with them on a visceral level much more than on a strategic level. The lesson is that strategy is important, but it is not something that people connect to personally. Purpose, however, is something to which people relate for one simple reason. It gives meaning to what they do. As Haudan says, it's that "larger than themselves" connection we all crave.

Part of engaging the workforce involves providing purpose, but that purpose must be put into a context of making things happen. One model for dynamism is agility. As defined by Thomas Williams, Christopher Worley, and Edward Lawler III, in an article for *strategy+business*, "Agility is not just the ability to change. It is a cultivated capability that enables an organization to respond in a timely, effective, and sustainable way when changing circumstances require it." According to the authors, agility is confirmed by four routines:

1. Strategizing dynamically—knowing what you do and why it matters
2. Perceiving environmental change—sensing that change is occurring and gauging its significance
3. Testing responses—assessing risk and learning from what has been happening
4. Implementing change—managing change to work for the organization

As Williams et al note, companies that possess the "agility factor" outperform their peers over the long term. Examples of such companies include ExxonMobil, Capital One, DaVita HealthCare Partners, and the Gap. The challenge for leaders is not to teach another business model, but to encourage managers and employees to make change work for them rather than against them. That emerges from having a shared purpose that everyone understands.[3]

As I wrote in my book, *Lead with Purpose*, when people know what is expected of them, they can deliver. Better yet, when they help contribute to those expectations, they may do even better. This means that managers need to make certain that people know that their place is to voice ideas when they have them, and—when appropriate and with approval—put them into gear. Such a culture of engagement is well-known at companies like 3M and Google, where employees are encouraged to devote time to pet projects that complement the mission of their teams as well as their organizations.[4]

Engagement: Setting the Foundation

For Ryan Lance, CEO of ConocoPhillips, engagement builds on purpose. Thus, all employees must know where the organization is headed. Lance shares his management philosophy with employees. It's a leadership concept he calls the SAM model: "The S stands for *set* directions. The A is *align*, and the M is *motivate*." As Lance explains, "When you can set a direction that's simple and inspiring—even differential—it really does motivate people, and they understand the strategic objectives of what you're trying to accomplish, where you're trying to go, and what they should expect from their leadership team."

As Lance notes, "It's absolutely critical that people understand the direction you're trying to go and leadership has to set the forward course, describe how the employees can connect and how their goals are contributing. Then you must energize stakeholders to get it done. We work really hard on alignment, and then spend a lot of time on motivation to make sure everybody is pulling the oars in the same direction."

Strategic intentions are built upon "a core set of values that set the tone for our direction and the behaviors needed," Lance said. "At ConocoPhillips, core values are expressed by the acronym SPIRIT. It stands for Safety, People, Innovation, Responsibility, Integrity, and Teamwork. The SPIRIT values summarize our character. Everything that we do reflects our SPIRIT values, both in our operations and in our interactions with the communities in which we operate. While we're fairly understated in how we approach things, our SPIRIT values always shine through."

Engagement Begins with Listening

Fernando Aguirre, former CEO of Chiquita Brands, believes that engagement relies upon two important factors: "One is to communicate all the time; and two is to find objectives that are common and that employees can make them their own." When Aguirre joined Chiquita as CEO, he spent his first ninety days as chairman and CEO "going on a listen and learn campaign and told employees that [he] was not going to make any major decisions in those first ninety days." Aguirre processed what he learned by writing about and reporting his findings to various business units.

The listening and learning continued throughout his tenure at Chiquita. Aguirre says, "I was very visible as the CEO of the company, and by that I mean I was walking around. I would do town hall meetings constantly. I was traveling anywhere between 60 and 80 percent of my time, depending on the time of the year. But anytime I would visit any of our operations, I would hold town hall meetings with every employee that was in the building, no matter what level, no matter if they had joined the day before or if they had been in the company thirty-five years. And I would talk a little bit about results. I would talk a little bit about what we were doing strategically, and then I would answer their questions. And I would spend anywhere between an hour and sometimes an hour and a half just talking to employees about what was going on in the operations."

Aguirre extended his town hall concept globally. He held quarterly review sessions that were broadcast throughout the company. He says, "I started every single town hall (or quarterly) meeting by reminding folks that the most important part of this session is going to be your questions." Employees were notified in advance to prepare questions.

Aguirre also leveraged his message to connect the corporate mission with the work that employees were doing. "You need to figure out objectives that are common for the majority of the people." As Aguirre explains, such commonality ensures that everyone is focused on the same goals, but it also enables managers to implement their own ideas in order to achieve the best results for their business units. In this way, Aguirre says it is employee "ideas that end up influencing the work."

Engagement: The Leader's Responsibility

Engagement is a process of setting the right example. People are always watching the leader. Her behavior becomes the yardstick by which others judge a leader. One way a leader can begin to set the right example is to be accessible and available.

As General John Allen explains, "The one area which I always felt was very important to my troops was that I was always present. I was always accessible. You have to stay up—you can't have bad days as a commander. You can't—while you may be under extreme pressure—show the pressure. And while there were a number of occasions where the enormity of what we were doing was really pressing in hard, if the commander is able to lead from the front—morally, spiritually, physically as well—but also tactically and operationally, the unit will hold together."

Keeping focused on the task at hand in trying circumstances means taking care of yourself. As Allen says, "One of the things that helped me a great deal is my endurance [which] is actually pretty good. It comes again from the ability to intrinsically motivate myself, and is based on my physical conditioning. [W]hen you're in good physical condition then you have the capacity to endure a great deal. You are less prone to uncertainty or less prone to the onset of fear. Your decisiveness is enhanced by your endurance."

That kind of fitness, certainly in a combat situation, gives those who follow the leader a kind of reassurance. "I'd be the last guy standing in a crisis and [our soldiers] took a lot of heart in that," says Allen. "They felt a substantial amount of comfort that, no matter how hard things got, the chances were pretty good that while I might be bent by the process it wasn't going to break me. That gave them a lot of confidence."

Endurance, however, cannot and should not be an excuse for trying to act superhuman. "Commanders and leaders need to take inventory of themselves—what are the personal conditions under which I'm operating right now," says Allen. "There were many occasions where I was simply exhausted, and exhausted day after day after day and one more crisis, the wash of one more crisis over me, I wondered whether I could take it or not." Honesty with oneself is essential to being able to engage with others. And that would sometimes means taking a nap. "If I could catch five, ten, or fifteen minutes in between events I'd lay down quickly and just close my eyes and get ten or fifteen minutes. We called it a 'combat nap.' But I'd fortify myself. I'd take inventory of where I am physically and spiritually and then immediately go about the business of ensuring that I was reacting to the crisis in a manner that calmed the command, not excited the command."

It's a leader's job to control his reaction to the situation or the crisis. "The last thing you need is for people to become excited in a crisis in a manner that compromises or in some way complicates decision making and the ability to react," says Allen. "You want to take the energy out of the crisis if you can, and insert the commander's calm. And in being calm in a crisis, it just permits everyone to face the issues and not face the energy, and that's really what you want to try to do."

John Allen's leadership behavior is a first-rate example of how a leader's behavior affects engagement. This is a topic that professor and author Jim Kouzes has studied. In analyzing data from the Leadership Practices Inventory, the leadership assessment that he codeveloped with Barry Posner, Kouzes found that the leader's behavior is the single biggest factor in determining workforce engagement. As Kouzes explains, "We can't predict engagement from knowing whether the workforce is highly educated or never attended college. We can't predict engagement based on whether the person is in marketing, finance, sales, or operations. We can't predict engagement if the constituents are male or female. We can't predict engagement based on any of these variables. Demographics accounts for less than 1 percent of the explained variance. But we can predict engagement based on how a leader behaves."

When it comes to engagement Kouzes says, "Leaders increase engagement at work when they are clear about their own personal values and when they make sure that people are aligned with shared values in the organization. Leaders increase engagement when they are also clear about where the team, business unit, or organization is headed, about the vision of the future. Leaders have to envision an uplifting and ennobling future and enlist others in it. We call that 'inspire a shared vision.' "

Kouzes also says that leaders increase engagement and performance when they "challenge the process, enable others to act, and encourage the heart." He and his coauthor find that when leaders more frequently demonstrate the Five Practices of Exemplary Leadership, as they refer to it, workforce engagement and performance go up. "There is no doubt," he says, "that exemplary leadership matters. The question is not, 'Do leaders make a difference?' They clearly do. The more important question is, 'How do leaders make a positive difference?' "

Engagement As Persuasion

Engagement begins with one-to-one contact. As basic as that sounds—and it *is* basic—too many leaders overlook it. One way to get a handle on engagement is to view it as an ongoing conversation with employees. And vital to engaging the interest of another is persuasion. For instance, Lyndon Johnson used his persuasion skills to help hold the nation together in the wake of the Kennedy assassination.

It is not simply a matter of talking a good game—though that helps—it really depends upon the ability to connect with other individuals. Masterful persuaders are those who can get inside the minds of the people they are seeking to persuade as a means of using that understanding to bring them around to their way of thinking.

As depicted in *The Passage of Power*, Volume 4 of Robert Caro's towering biography of the former president, Lyndon

Johnson was one such master of persuasion. He put his skills into high gear when he was thrust into the presidency at the "crack of a rifle," as contemporaries put it.[5] One example of his persuasive skills was his ability to get Richard Russell to serve on the Warren Commission investigating the Kennedy assassination. Although Russell was elderly and frail, he was much respected. Unfortunately, Russell disliked Chief Justice Earl Warren, who was heading the commission. The conversation between Johnson and Russell, recorded by the White House taping system and dissected in Caro's retelling, reveals the art of persuasion by an acknowledged master. Analysis of the recordings yields several useful strategies:

Do your homework. Johnson knew that Russell's participation on the committee would imbue it with a sense of dignity. At the same time, his loyalty to Johnson ensured that he would also be Johnson's eyes and ears, something that was vital to Johnson, who needed to be aware of the commission's doings.

Get inside the other person's head. Knowing what motivates the person you are seeking to persuade is essential. Russell was first and foremost a patriot, and Johnson leveraged that conviction by saying that Russell's participation on the committee was a national duty he could not ignore.

Focus your communication on the motivational factor. Tailor your communication to delivering what the other person is seeking: attention, recognition, or promotion. Johnson did this by playing on Russell's commitment to national service and his desire to help his former protégé, Johnson.

Highlight the importance of the other person. Make the person you are seeking to persuade acutely aware of how important she is to you and to the organization. Make her feel important in a constructive way. Johnson flattered Russell endlessly and it worked because Russell took pride in the younger man's praise.

Follow up. Never consider the persuasion complete until you have achieved your goal. You want the other person to support you and your project. Continue to employ the above steps to facilitate this. Johnson remained in close contact with Russell throughout his presidency and sought his counsel often.

Make no mistake, there may be elements of manipulation in persuasion. Johnson certainly manipulated Russell and a good many others. But effective persuaders are more than manipulators; they have core values that give them a foundation upon which to build their case. For Johnson, it was the fate of the republic. For executives it should be the fate of the individuals they lead.

Persuasion is a powerful tool that leaders use to bring people together for a common cause. Focusing your attention on it will enable you to reach the people you need, to bring them together for the good of the organization. Looked at from an organizational perspective, persuasion is a tool to stimulate engagement.

Mindful Engagement

While engagement is nurtured one on one, it will not work if the leader herself is not committed to the process. As Jim Haudan says, "The biggest mistake I hear leaders [make] is that they get up and they say...that the trains have left the station, the boats are sailing for a new destination, we're getting the right people on the right seats of the bus." According to Haudan, that kind of rhetoric does just the opposite: "People stay away from trains, boats, and company buses." Put another way, according to Haudan, too many managers view engagement as what you do *to* people rather than *for* them.

You need to make the personal connection. Haudan uses the analogy of successful comedians. He notes that Bill Cosby can have an audience of three thousand follow him after twelve minutes of watching him on stage. By contrast there are leaders with whom employees have worked for twelve years and they wouldn't cross the street for them. Why? Because according to Haudan, these executives "really don't understand the role of empathy" and the importance that empathy plays in validating an individual's sense of self-worth.

Personal connection to the work is critical. And that only occurs when leaders and followers are on the same wavelength. When they are both connected to the work and to the purpose, exciting things can happen.

Connect the Dots

The way to build upon personal connections is to "connect the dots." That is, the leader must relate the work of individuals to the collective work of the team and ultimately the organization. Adam Grant of Wharton notes that in organizations, particularly large ones, those who work in functional groups often do not see how their work links to the whole of the enterprise. His research shows that when you "[p]ut people in contact with the people who benefit from their efforts, you get a dramatic increase in motivation, performance, and productivity.... Engagement comes from recognizing that your work is meaningful and other people really value and appreciate it."

One example Grant cites is something that occurs at John Deere, the maker of farm equipment. The company stages something it calls the Golden Key ceremony, and it is for farmers and family members who are buying their first new tractor. Employees who helped assemble that tractor are invited to the ceremony to see the farmer take possession of the tractor by starting it for the first time. As Grant says, "The look of joy on the faces of the farmer and his family really brings the work to life." Employees know that such a tractor will be used in agriculture, so they take pride in the fact, says Grant, that "[t]hey are feeding a family and then all of the people" who will benefit from the farmer's labors. Chester Elton cites the example of Novartis Oncology. At an event inaugurating a new facility, leaders asked employees to sign their names on white tiles stating their dreams for the future of their function. One employee put it best when he wrote that his hope was to eradicate cancer and thereby abolish the need for their work. The white tiles were then turned into a sculpture and placed in the quad area where everyone could see it. There it stands as a testimony to the power of linking work to dreams and ultimately saving lives.

In medicine it is easy to link purpose to work, but what about a restaurant chain that sells steak and beer? As Elton told me, Texas Roadhouse has created Andy's Outreach, an employee assistance fund to which employees contribute and which the company matches. The funds are dispensed to employees in need. They even sell T-shirts promoting the cause. And taking the notion one step further, there is a Texas Roadhouse in Logan, Utah, that donates all profits, totaling more than $1 million a year, to the cause.

Philanthropy can be a key tool of engagement, as long as individual employees contribute willingly. A good example is The Cellular Connection (TCC), Verizon's largest premium retailer, with stores in more than thirty states. Headquartered in Carmel, Indiana, TCC has some nine hundred stores in thirty-four states. Scott Moorehead, president and CEO, believes in the philosophy of doing good by doing well.

"You have to take a step back and look what your values are," Moorehead said in a recent interview. "Then you can build your culture around that. Trying to force a culture that doesn't exist from a value perspective is impossible." As Moorehead says, "You have to build the culture you believe in, making it the first thing you filter all your decisions through."[6]

"When you put it together—customers matter, employees matter," says Moorehead. His original goal—and constant commitment—is "make a company where people want to come to work." One way to build on this commitment is to involve employees in giving back to the community.[7]

Such philosophy manifests itself in what TCC calls the "Culture of Good." The operating principle is giving back to others as a means of creating a workplace where employees are engaged in their work as well as engaged in their community. Each year the stores give away back-to-school backpacks for kids, and each store is encouraged to reach out to its local community to participate in charitable activities, either by making a donation or having associates donate their time. TCC employees have two paid days that they can use to participate in charitable activities.[8]

There is a sense of optimism that emerges from engagement with stakeholders, especially employees. While organizations foster optimism through their activities, leaders deliver it through actions. "Fundamentally," says Ryan Lance, CEO of ConocoPhillips, "I believe that people want to follow leaders who make them feel hopeful and take a positive view of the world. Optimism seems in short supply these days. So leaders who can bring people up—not bring them down—are just more inspiring to be around."

Engage with Your Presence

The way a leader engages people naturally comes down to an ability to hone her own behavior, or her presence. While the baseline for engagement must be the power of an idea, such as a cause or a goal, the leader must communicate individually and authentically. One example might be a musical conductor. In a delightful essay for the *Wall Street Journal*, Christopher Seaman delineates the ways that conductors can physically engage the musicians in an orchestra. The first is with the baton, typically held in the right hand, though there are lefties on the podium. The baton sets the tempo but is also a measure of expressiveness. The free hand either echoes the movement of the baton or underscores the music. For example, as Seaman writes, "a stroking cat" motion connotes sustained notes; a "chopping" motion does the opposite, calling for short, quick notes.

It is with the eyes that conductors truly connect. Arturo Toscanini, the great interpreter of Italian opera as well as Beethoven, had eyes that one conductor said could communicate the message without words. On a more human level, notes Seaman, a conductor's eyes radiate connection: "It gives individual players a strong sense of involvement." And if the conductor does not look their way, they tune him out and focus on their own interpretation.

If these techniques fail, the conductor can always fall back on his temper, letting flow with a volcano of insults designed to humiliate individuals and terrorize the entire orchestra. In truth, such displays of temper are more likely for show, and these days few musicians would pay much attention. They are professionals and want to be treated as such. So when faced with a conductor they do not respect, they do what all employees (or followers) do: pay him no mind.

But even with conducting there is the unknown, writes Seaman. "Conducting…is a very mysterious art," said conductor Carlo Maria Giulini. "I have no idea what I do up there." Fortunately, the musicians in the orchestra do, because Giulini, along with other great conductors, was known for his ability to bring a musical score to life, and more importantly, to breathe a spirit into it, creating great moments in music.[9]

Engagement, then, can be part physical. While a boss may not have a baton—or at least we hope not—she can use her presence as her instrument. That is, she makes time to be physically present. Picture an engaged school principal. She stands at the entrance of the school and greets students by name. I once watched a college president walk the hallways of his university, seemingly recognizing each and every person—student or faculty member—he saw. Watching him weave through a crowd was nearly magical, but it was also time-consuming. It took him three times as long to cross a room because he was connecting with so many people.

Time-consuming, sure, but it's a good use of time, because the leader is investing himself in the life of the organization. Physical presence is essential and lets people know they matter. Manifesting presence in one location is demanding, but global leaders face an even more daunting task, because the people they lead are scattered across continents. Leaders I know who have mastered engaging with a global workforce do it through electronic media, including video, and they also carve out time to visit employees wherever they are located.

While physical presence nurtures engagement, it is purpose—why we do what we do—that sustains it. And effective leaders use the power of purpose—getting things done to achieve intended results—to truly bring people together. And for that we can look to the example of an organization that has been around since the seventeenth century.

How the Royal Navy Keeps Itself Current

Engagement on a broad scale must be rooted in the values of the institution. A great example is set by Great Britain's Royal Navy. "Those who cannot remember the past," wrote philosopher George Santayana, "are condemned to repeat it." But, all too often, knowledge of institutional history can trap an organization in the status quo and mire it in mediocrity. And that is why long-standing institutions are finding ways to reinvigorate themselves while drawing strength from their legacies.

One such organization is Britain's Royal Navy. According to Andrew St. George, a management professor and author of *Royal Navy Way of Leadership*, this four-hundred-year-old institution keeps itself up-to-date by blending heritage with a responsibility to lead in the moment when duty calls.

An example of this lesson is a memorandum that Admiral Horatio Nelson wrote to captains of the ships in his armada shortly before the Battle of Trafalgar. While the memorandum contains plans for the battle, it also contains two admonitions: the first is, be prepared for the unexpected. As Nelson writes, "Something must be left to chance," since havoc rules in battle. The second is that captains are challenged to keep to the line, but should they become separated, Nelson adds encouragingly, "No captain can do very wrong if he places his ship alongside that of an enemy." As St. George notes, a senior officer in today's Royal Navy carries a laminated copy of Nelson's memorandum.

The Royal Navy nurtures its tradition through its culture. "The power of the Royal Navy approach is to focus on what individuals actually *did* in situations big and small," as St. George notes in an article for the *McKinsey Quarterly*, "thereby providing inspiration for new challenges while acknowledging that the nature of those challenges and leaders' responsibilities to them are an ever-changing, never ending story.'"

The Royal Navy drives its culture through engagement that focuses on morale, keeping sailors and marines in good cheer, which it fosters in games, in the mess, and in expeditionary exercises off the ship. In other words, it's one thing to talk a good game, but you have to instill pride through action and activity. And it works.

In the debrief to a serious flooding accident, the official inquiry report noted that "'morale remained high' throughout…and that 'teams remained cheerful and enthusiastic'…[and] 'sailors commented that the presence, leadership, and good humor of senior officers gave reassurance and confidence that the ship would survive.'"

What the Royal Navy does is not unique. I would argue that the U.S. Marines foster the same kind of institutional reverence balanced by the need to act independently while caring for fellow marines first and always. The question for those of us in the corporate sector is this: What can I do to foster this kind of balance? Let me offer three suggestions based on my observations in working with successful organizations.

1. *Revere the past, but do not be prisoner to it.* The challenge is to make your history work for you while making it crystal clear what each person must do to continue the mission. Tradition is preserved, but processes and procedures change. Allow employees to make changes that complement changing needs yet respect the values of the organization. That is, the phrase "It's the way we've always done it" must not become policy if needs and expectations change.

2. *Tell individual stories.* Organizations accomplish nothing; it's the people in them who do the work. Allow people to talk about what they have done

and why they did it. Hold "lessons learned" sessions after every major initiative. Invite employees to talk about what they would have done the same or differently. Use failure as a "teachable moment," not an attempt to shame or embarrass.

3. *Focus on engagement.* People do not work for institutions per se; they work with people. A leader's responsibility is to link the work of the individual employee to the mission of the organization. Demonstrate how the individual's work complements the team achievement. Hold people accountable for the good as well as the bad. Be liberal with good cheer and find ways to reward accomplishments.

It's no surprise that these are tenets borrowed from the Royal Navy, but you don't have to put on a uniform and swear allegiance to the queen to put them into practice. These principles apply to all types of organizations, including start-ups. Your history may be measured in decades rather than centuries, but in time you do accumulate experience. Very often the failures, if you pay attention closely, can be turned into lessons that will benefit the team and your customers if you make the adjustments and continue to improve.[10]

Make history work for you, not against you, and when you do, your legacy will be one that people integrate into their own future. Just as the Royal Navy has done for four centuries! History reinforces purpose.

Managing Without Bosses

Stimulating engagement can come from a fundamental reimagining of the way work gets done. This is an approach adopted by

Morning Star Company, the largest tomato processing company in the world, headquartered in Woodland, California. As profiled by management expert and author Gary Hamel, Morning Star is a place where bosses do not exist, corporate funds are spent by employees, no one has a title, and compensation is peer reviewed.

At Morning Star, employees are expected to be responsible for what they do to get the work done. As Hamel notes, they "[m]ake the mission the boss." In this way, people are focused on the task as well as on how that task complements the organization as a whole. According to Hamel there are six distinct advantages to the "management-free workplace."

1. *More initiative.* By defining work as the mission, people have the "authority to act." And they are recognized for what they do, too. People are engaged in the work.

2. *More expertise.* Quality is everyone's responsibility. "Experts aren't managers...they're people doing the work." In this way, expertise is applied where it matters most—where the work is done. (This is a fundamental concept behind *gemba*, a Japanese management technique in which value is derived from the workplace.)

3. *More flexibility.* Structure at Morning Star is like cloud formations that come and go. In other words, you apply the structure you need to do the job rather than have the job serve the structure, as it does in most organizations.

4. *More collegiality.* Without rank, or much of it, people feel freer to work better together. They collaborate to get the work done without looking to score points to advance their careers.

5. *Better judgment.* With work as the mission, the job comes first. Thinking about what the job is and how you can best do it enables people to make decisions that benefit the workflow. And Morning Star educates its workforce by providing them with courses in negotiation and financial analysis.

6. *More loyalty.* If you like thinking and doing for yourself in order to get the work done, Morning Star is a great place to work. People stick around. This even applies to seasonal workers who come to pick tomatoes.

Of course, the Morning Star approach is not for everyone. As Hamel notes, this self-management model presents difficulties. It takes time for people to fit in, and not everyone can adjust. Accountability can be an issue, as is an upward career path. What is applicable, however, is the possibility that work can be approached differently and employees can have more say in what they do in their jobs.[11]

Boss-less organizations can work well when the work is defined and execution is prized. A well-trained workforce can deliver on its objectives without constant supervision. But when creativity is needed, there is a need for a boss to create conditions where innovation can flourish. Such is the case with Menlo Innovations.

Fostering Engagement

At Menlo Innovations, employees work in an open-plan workplace. "No walls, offices, cubes, or doors. We work shoulder to shoulder," says CEO Rich Sheridan. "We all work in one environment that isn't spread out all over the planet. And we just think that's really important. We think that somewhere along the way we've lost our way as a society, when we think we can take human teams and spread them over multiple geographies and expect them to perform as well or as effectively as teams that are all sharing the same space together." Sheridan details his approach in his book, *Joy, Inc.: How We Built a Workplace People Love.*[12]

Menlo Innovations version of teamwork is the same kind of teamwork you see with sports teams. As Sheridan said in our interview, "They're on the field together. They're shoulder to shoulder...I don't think you get a team in the truest sense of the word until you've spent time together. And we've just chosen a different path because of our shared belief system."

This openness has the virtue of building esprit de corps, but it's not easy to keep running day to day, month to month. "Every day at Menlo, human beings walk in the door," says Sheridan. "They've got stuff going on at home. They've got stuff going on with their parents. They've got stuff going on with their children. They've got stuff going on with their friends. They've got stuff going on in their personal life, maybe with their health. All those things, as much as we'd like to believe get left at the door, don't. They're human beings. They can't possibly leave those things behind."

It falls to individuals to step up and resolve issues that threaten workplace harmony. Not everyone can do it, but over the years a culture has been established.

Engagement As Commitment

One element of engagement that many organizations overlook is commitment. Jim Haudan, CEO of Root, believes firmly that employees feel more engaged when the workplace is a place where they feel a sense of belonging. In part, this concept is derived from Haudan's approach of viewing employees as customers. Adopting this mind-set shifts the balance from what *we do to* an employee to what *we can do for* them. Making the personal connection between the employee and the work is vital to engagement, but more importantly, it creates a bond between the employee and the enterprise. Once an employee feels connected, she will go the extra mile to achieve intended results.

At Root, management fosters commitment in a variety of ways. One method is borrowed from something that Haudan witnessed at a ceremony at Lourdes University in Ohio. Freshmen at the school are given a ceramic medallion. When they graduate, they give the medallion to the person at the school who helped them the most. Haudan adapted that concept to recognize employees. Employees were given a tree and then asked to give that tree to the person who had meant the most to him and helped him feel part of the Root organization.

The team at Menlo Innovations does something similar. Sheridan says, "We have group sessions, quarterly meetings, to talk about the business, or lunch and learn around some concept that we're working on. And quite frankly, there are times when what we discuss is difficult, [when there is] some aspect of the team we want to make improvements to and we're talking about it. You can start to see that some people are bristling a little bit because they think it should go one way and other people are bristling another way because they think it should go their way."

It is important not to let the meeting end on a down note, so Menlo has adopted a practice that Zingerman's, one of the world's premier food companies (also headquartered in Ann Arbor), uses. It's called "Appreciates." As Sheridan says, "It's like a popcorn type of commentary at the end where somebody will say, 'You know what? I really *appreciate* that despite the fact that we were talking through some very difficult concepts that everybody here was willing to raise their voice and let it be known what's on their mind.' And somebody else will say, 'I really *appreciate* when my colleague shared with us how she was feeling when this happened.' And somebody else says, 'I really appreciate that we have an environment here that we foster that allows us to come together.' And boy, you do that at the end of a meeting and no matter how difficult the conversation was everybody walks away with this incredibly warm feeling about each other, about themselves, and about the whole team. It is magical."

There is something else that Haudan believes in—humor. At Root, there is a practice called Rooties and Tooties. Rooties are awarded for good work, like the Oscars. A Tootie is a spoof of a fellow employee. For example, Haudan has been lampooned by staffers for being too long-winded in his presentations or for not really doing any work; they joke that he has his executive assistant do everything. By encouraging such comedy, the company breaks down barriers, and people treat one another as people. Informality is important.

Fun is important, and whatever method you choose, it is a means of making a connection from one person to another. Such a connection facilitates commitment to the work, but also to colleagues and even bosses. This is fundamental to stimulating and growing engagement.

Engagement can mean many things to many people but, bottom line, it can be summed up by the desire to create a workplace atmosphere where people feel appreciated and are motivated to do good work.

Closing Thought: Engagement

A leader is more than a sum of what he has accomplished. A leader is judged by how well he enabled others to achieve their aims in ways that benefit the entire organization. That is the essence of engagement—bringing people together for common purpose.

When people are united in purpose they can accomplish things together that they might not have thought possible. And that's the secret of positive engagement. People apply their own skills, individually and collectively, in order to achieve desired and sustainable results.

Engagement = People + Commitment

Leadership Questions

- What are you doing to connect more effectively with others?
- What do you think you could be doing better?
- What changes will you make so that you make personal connections a key priority?

Leadership Directives

- Engagement is the process of connecting one person to another. Learn to work with and for others as a means of achieving mutually beneficial goals.
- The first form of engagement is communication. Use your words to initiate a connection but follow through on that connection with positive actions.
- Our behavior sets the tone for how others will regard us. Adopt a perspective of seeking to assist rather than to confront or disrupt. This approach promotes greater openness.

- We reinforce engagement through our actions: consider how well you reach out to others, listen to what they have to say, and pay attention to their ideas.
- Lead with a sense of inclusiveness. That is, keep people informed with news, apprised of the situation, and engaged in the work.

Appendix

Your Moxie Handbook: Making Moxie Work for You

Individuals with moxie, as we have seen in this book, are those who seek to make a positive difference in their own lives as well as the lives of those around them. Leaders with moxie are those with the courage to be counted, the get-up-and-go to take action, and the desire to get recognition for their teams as well as themselves.

This handbook will provide you with action steps you can apply to make moxie work for you. Part 1 focuses on motivation; part 2 provides motivational advice from the experts I have quoted throughout this book; and part 3 concentrates on actions suggested by the chapters in this book.

Motivation = Desire + Willpower

Part 1: Self-Motivation

Leaders by nature focus on things around them rather than on themselves, which is why mindfulness techniques are useful. There is something else leaders need to do because the organization expects it: they must be motivated, driven to push forward as well as to develop their skills and their talents. Typically, leaders are good at pushing, but sometimes they ignore their own needs, and one of them is maintaining their energy level—physically, mentally, and spiritually.

Here are some suggestions.

To keep your body energized...

- Exercise when possible. I know many executives who go out of their way to keep fit, even when travel and time push against them. If you cannot get to your local gym or personal exercise room, go for a run or practice calisthenics in your hotel room.

- Eat right. All things in moderation, as my physician father used to say. That includes alcohol as well as foods that may be tasty but not as good for us as, say, vegetables or tofu.

To keep your mind energized...

- Visit your employees. Make certain you go to where people work. Adopt their perspective when they approach a job. It will give you a different point of view about how well things are going or not going.

- Keep in touch with customers. These folks are the ones you are in business to serve. Find ways to learn how they use your products and services.

- Know your competition. The urge to compete likely emerges from deep within our genetic code. It's part of self-preservation. Learn from what your competitors do right as well as what they do poorly.

- Keep up with the literature in your field. This is typically not too difficult because it is always readily available.

- Read for pleasure. This is hard for some, because if you work long hours and read material in your discipline, it can be hard to find time to open a book. Yet many executives do it. Read what you enjoy—fiction, biographies, history, military history. All of these topics stimulate our minds.

- Travel for pleasure. Visit places that are new and different. When we are in new places, we take in sights, sounds, and smells that are unfamiliar. They awaken our senses and keep us alert.

To keep your spirit energized...

- Reflect. Make time to gain perspective on the day. You can do it solo or with a trusted colleague. (See more suggestions in the Mindfulness section in part 3.)

- Meditate. Some leaders like to practice meditation. I have friends who meditate for thirty minutes a day. Others find five quiet moments to sit back and empty their minds of thoughts. It is a way of shutting out the outside world and getting in touch with your inner self.

Part 2: Advice from the Experts

Understand What Makes You Tick
Ryan Lance, CEO, ConocoPhillips

Ryan Lance credits his upbringing with molding him into the individual he is today.

Growing up on a farm with pretty significant role models like my father and grandfather taught me a strong work ethic and pride in my work—kind of a mental toughness. But more importantly, it taught me humility. I like to win, but certainly not at all costs.

I approach business with many of the same lessons from my early life. I want to be part of creating something that brings out the best in others. I want to be known for high ethical standards and a core set of moral values. And I think that gets enhanced and multiplied by a passion and love for what I do.

Build Your Dream
Rich Sheridan, cofounder and CEO, Menlo Innovations and author of *Joy, Inc.*

Rich Sheridan's inclination toward entrepreneurship began early.

I loved to make things, whether it was just from scraps of lumber or Lego blocks or erector sets. I think there was that inner engineer in me that delighted not only in building things, but building things that delighted other people. That's sort of a core of my existence to build things that delight other people, that sort of moment when you're a kid where maybe your parents looked at something you made and were like, "Wow, that's amazing. How did you do that?"

The real delight...[was that] I always wanted to work on something for other people, for something maybe bigger than myself over time. And that's where a lot of the motivation came from.

But there were moments in my career, long moments, where that was not happening, where I was very frustrated, because I felt a barrier between me and those things that I was trying to help bring to the world that would delight people. And that shifted my motivation to better understanding how to create a system for delivering those kind of results over and over again.

Know What You Like to Do
Jim Kouzes, Dean's Executive Fellow of Leadership, Leavey School of Business at Santa Clara University; coauthor with Barry Posner of more than thirty books and workbooks, including *The Leadership Challenge*

Lifelong learning has shaped Jim Kouzes' outlook on life and career.

I love to learn. And I do what I do because I get to learn something new every day. It is really what motivates me to keep doing what I'm doing.... I make a daily habit of reading and learning. I set aside two hours every morning. That's how I stay current in the field. Learning requires discipline and self-motivation. You have to make the time and space to do it.

Don't Be Afraid to Take Risks
Donald Altman, MA, LPC, psychotherapist; best-selling author of *The Mindfulness Code* and *One-Minute Mindfulness*

Donald Altman, psychotherapist, counsels others to delve into their consciousness. He follows his own advice.

I was willing to move into areas where I was uncomfortable, and that helped me succeed in ways I couldn't have imagined. And I think that we all need to allow ourselves to evolve and to grow in areas that are not necessarily our strengths. And when we do that it can open up new avenues and new understandings of ourselves that allow us to go past thinking, "Oh, I can't do that" or "I can't do this." [As we say] "Necessity is the mother of invention." But necessity is also what can help us grow and provide us some of the greatest opportunities in our lives.

Know Your Background
General John Allen, USMC (retired), Commander of NATO forces in Afghanistan (2009–2011) and special deputy for the Middle East for Secretary of State John Kerry

For General John Allen, history is a motivator socially. History is also personal to Allen who together with his wife's family comes from a tradition totaling over 100 years of service:

> History for [Marines] is almost genealogical in a sense. Keeping faith with our traditions, keeping faith with our service, keeping faith with each other as marines, *semper fidelis,* which is always faithful, is not something that is lightly used or exchanged between marines as a matter of our history.... I also have a pretty substantial sense of my family history, which I try to keep faith with, but also my personal religious faith as well. So all of those things are intrinsic to my doing my duty.

Make Things Happen
Fernando Aguirre, former CEO, Chiquita Brands

Fernando Aguirre believes that if you want to succeed you must try to make things happen. Growing up in Mexico City, he was a star baseball player and played on the winning national teams three times between the ages of twelve and fifteen. His ambitions, however, extended beyond baseball. He wanted to learn English so he could one day study in the United States. Says Aguirre:

What I did at seventeen years old was very adven-
turesome in those days. You didn't hear of foreign
exchange student that much then. I worked for a year
with my grandfather selling cars, or I thought I was selling cars, and I saved and paid the equivalent of $750
to become a foreign exchange student for one year. My
parents couldn't pay for it and I went in one day to my
parents and I said, "I'm going to the U.S." And they
said, "No, you're not because we can't pay for it." I said,
"I've already paid for it." And they couldn't believe it.
And I put my 750 bucks in and bought my year of being
abroad, and it probably was the best decision I've ever
made in my life.

Conquer Your Fears
Adam Grant, professor of management, University of Pennsylvania Wharton School and author of *Give and Take*

Adam Grant was a competitive diver in his youth. It was not
easy because Grant was afraid of heights, and the idea of standing at the edge of a tall platform made him nervous. But he persevered, even advancing to the U.S. Olympic trials one year. He
also faced another fear in his post-diving life. Fears do not dis-
sipate by themselves. It requires practice and often the expertise
of coaches and mentors, which Grant credits with helping him
become a better diver and eventually an accomplished public
speaker:

> As somebody who is afraid of heights and afraid of
> public speaking leaping off a thirty-three-foot, nine-inch
> platform to hit the water at thirty-five miles an hour was
> a lot scarier and overcoming that was great preparation
> for getting more comfortable on stage.

Desire to Help
Doug Conant, former CEO of Campbell's Soup and best-selling
author of *TouchPoints*

Often, you can motivate yourself by looking at how you can be
of assistance to others This approach is one that Doug Conant
draws upon.

> I have found that what keeps me in the game all the
> time is bringing forward a "How can I help?" attitude to
> every engagement and to every issue. And that leads me
> to a place where I'm trying to be very mindful of what's
> going on so I can find a way to add value to the situation.

Never Stop Believing in Yourself
Jim Haudan, CEO, Root, Inc.; author of *The Art of Engagement*

Jim Haudan believes deeply that leaders must commit to their
work as well as their people. The key words are *faith*, *fire*, and
focus.

> FAITH...Faith in my ability to excel, to contrib-
> ute, to be a champion. A champion is someone who
> believes in themselves when no one else does. FAITH is
> also the deep belief that the only one that could keep me
> off the field is me...and the only one who could get me
> on the field is me.
> FIRE is passion...that intangible ingredient that
> trumps all else. If life was a game of rock, paper, and
> scissors...passion is the wild card. Passion wins over
> skill. It beats out better ideas, and it outruns com-
> monly accepted stopping points. Passion has no accepted
> boundaries.
> FOCUS is the relentless preparation, the flawless

success routines, and to the exclusion of all else...envisioning only the successful outcome.

Because limits like fears are often Illusions... FAITH...FIRE...and FOCUS are the "Illusion Busters."[1]

See the Future As a Possibility
Mark Goulston, MD, founder Heartfelt Leadership and author of *Just Listen* and *Get Out of Your Own Way at Work*

Mark Goulston is a keen observer and as such his powers of observation coupled with his deep perception provide him with insights from which others draw wisdom.

I think what motivates me is being able to see the "hidden-in-plain-sight" elephant in the room that stands in the way of progress and at the other end is the gateway to breakthrough opportunity and success. When I work with people I seem to be able to listen and describe a future and a personal brand that they love of the idea of living. The proof that you have arrived at such a potential vision is that they break eye contact with you, look up at the ceiling to ponder what you and they are talking about, then they look back at you with a smile and say, "Do you really think that's possible? Could I really do and be that?" The fact that it really floats their boat is not a bad start.

Cherish Your Family
Chester Elton, the "Apostle of Appreciation" and coauthor with Adrian Gostick of *The Carrot Principle, The Orange Revolution,* and *All In*

Chester Elton believes strongly in family. His own is closely knit and from it he draws comfort and strength.

I think when you've got a family and kids, you're very motivated to pay your mortgage. But it's really interesting. The way I've always done it is I've always looked at how grateful I was to be where I was, how lucky I was to be where I was, and that there were so many people who would trade places with me. To never take it for granted and to always make sure that I represented not only the company that I worked for well, but that I represented my family and my family name. Those were always great motivators for me, to really be grateful but to understand that I didn't get here just by luck. That there were a lot of people who contributed to my success and I have great motivation to never let those people down. So I always want to give my best every day.

The good leaders I've found take the great principles that build good teams at work and help [their employees] build good families at home. It really does help. It's so funny. We've got all these great principles to create all these great teams at work and then these guys go home and their families are completely dysfunctional. I say, "You idiot. Take what you have learned at work and apply it at home! And what you learn at home bring it to work!

Part 3: Action Steps

Mindfulness—*being aware of the world around you*

- Take stock of your situation every day. Ask yourself what is happening, as well as what is not happening.

- Look for ways to teach others to be mindful of the way they interact with colleagues. Setting the right example is the best way to teach.

- Find ways to exercise patience. Remember, patience is an act of control. You cannot control the situation, but you can control how you react to it.

- Make time to enjoy something simple every day: your morning coffee, your daily exercise, or your walk to a favorite spot. Savor the moment.

Opportunity—*seeing potential where others see only problems*

- Look for challenges facing your team. Ask yourself what it will take to address them.

- Examine the obstacles. Are they real or imagined? Can you overcome them with the right resources?

- Ask yourself what ventures are worth pursuing and why. Stretching too far may overextend your team.

- Consider the talent on your team. Do you have the right people in the right places to succeed? If not, do you need to provide further training and development opportunities?

- Be realistic. Every obstacle does not need to be overcome. Sometimes it is best to walk away. Husband your resources for future challenges.

X factor—*demonstrating the "right stuff of leadership"*

- Character is fundamental to leadership. Is the example you set rooted in integrity?

- How are you channeling ambition? For yourself or for your team?

- Creativity is essential to thinking differently. Are you providing yourself the right stimuli to keep your creative flame lit?

- How are you demonstrating resilience? Resourceful leaders do not give up right away. They persevere. And while they cannot succeed all of the time, the way they battle adversity radiates their character.

- Are you finding ways to insist on integrity in your team? Strong organizations practice their values in such a way that they make it almost hard for employees to make a wrong ethical choice. This does not mean they are perfect; it means that they practice their values so that people are rewarded for doing what is right rather than what is expedient.

Innovation—*thinking and doing differently*

- Teams that innovate must do so in an environment where ideas are wanted.

- Consider the obstacles that are hindering innovation in your team. Obstacles could be resources, time, or even management. What can you do to overcome such obstacles?

- Artists in Venice's famed Murano glassblowing district are invited to "think in glass." Consider how you are applying that idea to your team. Are you encouraging them to think new and differently?[2]

- Are you enabling people to apply lessons from the past (even the very recent past) to solve problems that are vexing your team right now?

- How are you building a culture of innovation? That is, are you making it safe for people to fail—as long as they fail the "right way." This means people are trying new things that complement—and do not hinder—what the organization is trying to accomplish.

Engagement—*viewing others as contributors and collaborators*

- As a leader, you can't accomplish much of anything alone. You need the talents and skills of others.

- Consider how you treat your teammates. Are they people with whom you *want to* work, or people with whom you *have to* work? How can you change the dynamic?

- How do you let people know that you regard them as contributors? Do you recognize their work or do you ignore it until something goes wrong?

- Consider what collaboration means. To be successful, collaborators often combine their ideas to create something that is greater than the sum of its parts. This involves a sacrifice in pride of authorship perhaps. What kind of a contributor are you? What can you do differently?

- What steps are you taking to encourage collaboration? Are you setting the right example yourself? That is, are you asking people to do what you are not willing to do?

Notes

Note: All interview comments from experts are taken from interviews with the author conducted in Fall 2013.

Chapter 1

1. *2013 Best Companies for Leadership,* Hay Group, 2013, http://www.hay group.com/bestcompaniesforleadership/media-fact-box/index.aspx. The Best Companies for Leadership Study, developed by the Hay Group, surveyed nearly 18,000 individuals at more than 2,200 organizations worldwide. The 2013 study is the eighth in an annual series that began in 2006.
2. Adapted from the following sources: John Carlin, *Playing for the Enemy: Nelson Mandela and the Game That Made a Nation* (New York: Penguin, 2008); *Invictus,* directed by Clint Eastwood and written by Anthony Peckham, starring Morgan Freeman and Matt Damon, 2009.
3. John Baldoni, "Few Executives Have Self-Awareness but Women Do Better," *Harvard Business Review* (May 9, 2013), http://blogs.hbr .org/2013/05/few-executives-are-self-aware/.
4. Baldoni, "Few Executives Have Self-Awareness but Women Do Better."
5. 2012 Hay Group Study based upon review of Emotional and Social Competency Index, http://www.businesswire.com/news/home/201203 27005180/en#.UxS0-9wrd00; also Baldoni, "Few Executives Have Self-Awareness but Women Do Better," http://blogs.hbr.org/2013/05/ few-executives-are-self-aware/.
6. Donald Altman's reference to Velcro comes from neuropsychologist Rick Hanson, who said, "Your brain is like Velcro for negative experiences and Teflon for positive ones—even though most of your experiences are probably neutral or positive...and in relationships, it typically takes about five positive interactions to overcome the effects of a single negative one," Donald Altman, *One-Minute Mindfulness* (Novato, CA: New World Library, 2011), 30.

7. JoelStein"TheRealTerminator:HowJerryBrownScaredCaliforniaStraight," *Bloomberg/Businessweek* (May 5, 2103), http://www.businessweek.com/articles/2013-04-25/jerry-brown-californias-grownup-governor.
8. Stein, "The Real Terminator: How Jerry Brown Scared California Straight."
9. Stein, "The Real Terminator: How Jerry Brown Scared California Straight."
10. Stein, "The Real Terminator: How Jerry Brown Scared California Straight."
11. Stein, "The Real Terminator: How Jerry Brown Scared California Straight."
12. *Lincoln*, written by Anthony Kushner and directed by Steven Spielberg, 2012.
13. Dan Damon, "Judith Tebbutt: My Six Months Held Hostage by Somali Pirates," *BBC News Magazine* (July 26, 2013); See also Judith Tebbutt, *A Long Walk Home* (London: Faber and Faber, 2013).
14. Doris Kearns Goodwin, *Team of Rivals: The Political Genius of Abraham Lincoln* (New York: Simon & Schuster, 2005).

Chapter 2

1. *2013 Best Companies for Leadership*, Hay Group, 2013, http://www.haygroup.com/bestcompaniesforleadership/media-fact-box/index.aspx.
2. David Barrett, *Miracle at Merion: The Inspiring Story of Ben Hogan's Comeback and Win at the 1950 U.S. Open* (New York: Skyhorse Publishing, 2010), 285–86.
3. Based on Curt Sampson, *Hogan* (New York: Broadway Books, 1997); David Barrett, *Miracle at Merion: The Inspiring Story of Ben Hogan's Comeback and Win at the 1950 U.S. Open* (New York: Skyhorse Publishing, 2010).
4. James M. Kouzes and Barry Z. Posner, *The Leadership Challenge: How to Make Extraordinary Things Happen in Organizations*, Fifth Edition (New York: Jossey-Bass, 2012).
5. Susan Berfield, "Why the McWrap Is So Important to McDonald's," *Bloomberg Businessweek* (July 3, 2013).
6. Ashlee Vance, "Electric Car Company Chic," *Bloomberg/Businessweek*, July, 28, 2013; Ashlee Vance, "Elon Musk: The 21st. Century Industrialist," *Bloomberg Businessweek* (September 13, 2012).
7. David Carr, "TV Foresees Its Future. Netflix Is There," *New York Times* (July 22, 2013).
8. Adam Hartung, "Netflix: The Turnaround Story of 2012," Forbes.com (January 29, 2013), http://www.forbes.com/sites/adamhartung/2013/01/29/netflix-the-turnaround-story-of-2012/.
9. Carr, "TV Foresees Its Future. Netflix Is There."
10. Carr, "TV Foresees Its Future. Netflix Is There."

11. Susan Dominus, "Is Giving the Secret to Getting Ahead?" *New York Times Magazine* (March 27, 2013); Adam Grant, *Give and Take: Revolutionary Approach to Success* (New York: Viking, 2013).
12. Daniel Isenberg, *Worthless, Impossible, and Stupid: How Contrarian Entrepreneurs Create and Capture Extraordinary Value* (Boston: Harvard Business Review Press 2013) 142.
13. Isenberg, *Worthless, Impossible, and Stupid*, 144–151.
14. Isenberg, *Worthless, Impossible, and Stupid*, 179–189, 193–210.
15. Isenberg, *Worthless, Impossible, and Stupid*, 208–210.

Chapter 3

1. Matt Paese, "Why Executives React: Personality Patterns that Survive at the Top" Developmental Dimensions International, Inc. (2013) http://www.ddiworld.com/DDIWorld/media/pov/whyexecutivesreact_pov_ddi.pdf?ext=.pdf
2. Adapted from the following materials: "A Look at Thatcherism, the Polarizing Legacy of the 'Iron Lady' " with Gwen Ifill (host), John Burns (*New York Times*), and Rana Foroohar *(Time)*, PBS NewsHour (April 9, 2013); Joseph R. Gregory, "'Iron Lady' Who Set Britain on a New Course," *New York Times* (April 8, 2013); Alistair MacDonald, "Former British Prime Minister Margaret Thatcher Dies," *Wall Street Journal* (April 8, 2013); David Brooks, "The Vigorous Virtues," *New York Times*, April 9, 2013; A.C. Grayling, "Thatcher's Divided Isle," *New York Times* (April 9, 2013). Additionally, this profile drew inspiration from three fictional films: *The Iron Lady* (2011*)* starring Meryl Streep, written by Abi Morgan and directed by Phyllida Lloyd; *Margaret Thatcher: The Long Walk to Finchley* (2008), produced by Robert Cooper, Kate Triggs, Bethan Jones, BBC Films; *Margaret* (2009) written by Richard Cottan and directed by James Kent BBC Films.
3. Jeffrey Kruger, "Assessing the Creative Spark," Time.com (May 9, 2013). Survey data drawn from infographic based upon research by the Time/MPAA/Microsoft Survey conducted by Penn Shoen Berland, April 2013, No. 2040 adult consumers, http://business.time.com/2013/05/09/assessing-the-creative-spark/.
4. Howard Gardner *Frames of Mind: Theory of Multiple Intelligences,* Third Edition (New York: Basic Books, 2011); Howard Gardner, *Multiple Intelligences: New Horizons in Theory and Practice* (New York: Basic Books, 2006).
5. John Baldoni, "5 Questions Every Leader Needs to Ask," Forbes.com (September 17, 2013), http://www.forbes.com/sites/johnbaldoni/2013/09/

17/character-5-questions-to-ask-yourself/. The questions emerged from comments made by Jeff Nelson, director of OneGoal, quoted in Joe Nocera, "Reading, Math and Grit," *New York Times* (September 7, 2012).

6. John Baldoni, "Ronald Reagan's Secret to Great Leadership," FastCompany.com (February 11, 2011), http://www.fastcompany.com/1725652/ronald-reagans-secret-great-leadership.

7. Thomas J. Figueira, T. Corey Brennan, and Rachel Hall Sternberg, *Wisdom from the Ancients* (New York: Perseus Publishing, 2001), 206–7; Alexander the Great, https://en.wikipedia.org/wiki/Alexander_the_Great.

Chapter 4

1. *2013 Best Companies for Leadership,* Hay Group, 2013, http://www.haygroup.com/bestcompaniesforleadership/media-fact-box/index.aspx.

2. Adapted from Jennifer Clark, *Mondo Agnelli: Fiat, Chrysler, and the Power of a Dynasty* (Hoboken, NJ: John Wiley & Sons, 2011); John Baldoni, "What It Takes to Lead a Turnaround," CBSNews Moneywatch, (January 24, 2012).

3. Drew Boyd and Jacob Goldenberg, "Think Inside the Box," *Wall Street Journal*, (June 14, 2013).

4. "Innovation Pessimism," *The Economist* (January 12, 2013).

5. "Innovation Pessimism," *The Economist.*

6. Robert J. Gordon, "Why Innovation Won't Save Us," *Wall Street Journal* (December 21, 2012).

7. Boyd and Goldenberg, "Think Inside the Box."

8. "Titans of Innovation," Schumpeter, *The Economist,* (April 27, 2013).

9. Brad Stone, "Inside Google's Secret Lab," *Bloomberg Businessweek* (May 22, 2013).

10. "Venetian Glass: Blow Up," *The Economist,* (July 6, 2013).

Chapter 5

1. *2013 Best Companies for Leadership,* Hay Group, 2013, http://www.haygroup.com/bestcompaniesforleadership/media-fact-box/index.aspx.

2. Adapted from Dolly Parton entry, Biography.com; "Country Music Legend Dolly Parton's New Role: 'Book Lady,'" PBS *NewsHour* (May 29, 2013); Dana McMahan, "Dollywood to Get $300 Million Upgrade," *Today* (August 21, 2013); John Baldoni, "The Leadership Lessons of Dolly Parton," HBR.org (March 25, 2008).

3. Thomas Williams, Christopher G. Worley, and Edward E. Lawler, "The Agility Factor," *strategy+business* (April 15, 2013).
4. John Baldoni, *Lead with Purpose: Giving Organizations a Reason to Believe in Themselves* (New York: AMACOM, 2011), 66–70.
5. Robert Caro, *Lyndon Johnson: The Passage of Power,* vol 4. (New York: Alfred A. Knopf, 2012), 446–51.
6. Dennis Seeds, "Scott Moorehead Uses Culture to Drive Success at The Cellular Connection to the Tune of $600 Million in Sales," *SmartBusiness/Indianapolis* (November 24, 2013).
7. Seeds, "Scott Moorehead Uses Culture to Drive Success at The Cellular Connection to the Tune of $600 Million in Sales."
8. Seeds, "Scott Moorehead Uses Culture to Drive Success at The Cellular Connection to the Tune of $600 Million in Sales."
9. Christopher Seaman, "What Is That Conductor Up To?" *Wall Street Journal* (August 3, 2013).
10. Andrew St. George, "Leadership Lessons from the Royal Navy," *McKinsey Quarterly* (January 2013). See also Andrew St. George, *Royal Navy Way of Leadership* (London: Cornerstone Publishing, June 2012).
11. Gary Hamel "First, Let's Fire All the Managers," *Harvard Business Review* (December 2011). [For more information on this approach, read Gary Hamel, *What Matters Now* New York: Jossey-Bass, 2012).
12. Richard Sheridan, *Joy, Inc.: How We Built a Workplace People Love* (New York: Portfolio/Penguin, 2014).

Appendix

1. Jim Haudan's comments excerpted from "Blake's Story," a presentation about overcoming adversity. Used with permission. The theme "Faith, Fire, and Focus" is attributed to the author and consultant Alan Fine, www.alan-fine.com.
2. "Venetian Glass: Blow Up," *The Economist* (July 6, 2013).

References

"2013 Best Companies for Leadership." Hay Group, 2013. http://www.haygroup.com/bestcompaniesforleadership/media-fact-box/index.aspx.

"A Look at Thatcherism, the Polarizing Legacy of the 'Iron Lady.'" With Gwen Ifill (host), John Burns, and Rana Foroohar, *PBS/NewsHour*, April 9, 2013.

Altman, Donald. *One Minute Mindfulness*. Novato, CA: New World Library, 2011.

Baldoni, John. "5 Questions Every Leader Needs to Ask." Forbes.com, September 17, 2013. http://www.forbes.com/sites/johnbaldoni/2012/09/17/character-5-questions-to-ask-yourself/.

————. "Few Executives Have Self-Awareness but Women Do Better." *Harvard Business Review*, May 9, 2013. http://blogs.hbr.org/2013/05/few-executives-are-self-aware/.

————. "What It Takes to Lead a Turnaround." CBSNews Moneywatch, January 24, 2012.

————. *Lead with Purpose: Giving Organizations a Reason to Believe in Themselves*. New York: AMACOM, 2011.

————. "Ronald Reagan's Secret to Great Leadership," FastCompany.com, February 11, 2011. http://www.fastcompany.com/1725652/ronald-reagans-secret-great-leadership.

————. "The Leadership Lessons of Dolly Parton." HBR.org, March 25, 2008.

Barrett, David. *Miracle at Merion: The Inspiring Story of Ben Hogan's Comeback and Win at the 1950 U.S. Open*. New York: Skyhorse Publishing, 2010.

Berfield, Susan. "Why the McWrap Is So Important to McDonald's." *Bloomberg/Businessweek*, July, 3, 2013.

Boyd, Drew, and Jacob Goldenberg. "Think Inside the Boss." *Wall Street Journal*, June 14, 2013.

Brooks, David. "The Vigorous Virtues." *New York Times*, April 9, 2013.

Carlin, John. *Playing for the Enemy: Nelson Mandela and the Game That Made a Nation*. New York: Penguin, 2008.

Caro, Robert. *The Passage of Power: The Years of Lyndon Johnson, Vol 4.* New York: Alfred A. Knopf, 2012.

Carr, David. "TV Foresees Its Future. Netflix Is There." *New York Times,* July 22, 2013.

Clark, Jennifer. *Mondo Agnelli: Fiat, Chrysler, and the Power of a Dynasty.* Hoboken, NJ: John Wiley & Sons, 2011.

"Country Music Legend Dolly Parton's New Role: 'Book Lady,'" PBS *News-Hour,* May 29, 2013.

Damon, Dan. "Judith Tebbutt: My Six Months Held Hostage by Somali Pirates." *BBC News Magazine,* July 26, 2013.

"Dolly Parton Biography." Biography.com. http://www.biography.com/people/dolly-parton-9434112#awesm=~oI2O1oumeWrMZi.

Dominus, Susan. "Is Giving the Secret to Getting Ahead?" *The New York Times Magazine,* March 27, 2013.

Figueira, Thomas J., T. Corey Brennan, and Rachel Hall Sternberg. *Wisdom from the Ancients.* New York: Perseus Publishing, 2001.

Gardner, Howard. *Frames of Mind: Theory of Multiple Intelligences,* Third Edition. New York: Basic Books 2011.

————. *Multiple Intelligences: New Horizons in Theory and Practice.* New York: Basic Books, 2006.

Gordon, Robert J. "Why Innovation Won't Save Us." *Wall Street Journal,* December 21, 2012.

Grant, Adam. *Give and Take: Revolutionary Approach to Success.* New York: Viking, 2013.

Grayling, A.C. "Thatcher's Divided Isle." *New York Times,* April 9, 2013.

Gregory, Joseph R. "'Iron Lady' Who Set Britain on a New Course." *New York Times,* April 9, 2013.

Hamel, Gary. "First, Let's Fire All the Managers." *Harvard Business Review,* December 2011.

————. *What Matters Now.* New York: Jossey-Bass, 2012.

Hartung, Adam. "Netflix: The Turnaround Story of 2012," Forbes.com, January 29, 2013. http://www.forbes.com/sites/adamhartung/2013/01/29/netflix-the-turnaround-story-of-2012/.

Invictus. Written by Anthony Peckham and directed by Clint Eastwood. Starring Morgan Freeman and Matt Damon, 2009.

Iron Lady. Written by Abi Morgan and directed by Phyllida Lloyd. Starring Meryl Streep, 2011.

"Innovation Pessimism," *The Economist,* January 12, 2013.

Isenberg, Daniel. *Worthless, Impossible, and Stupid: How Contrarian Entrepreneurs Create and Capture Extraordinary Value.* Boston: Harvard Business Review Press, 2013.

Kearns Goodwin, Doris. *Team of Rivals: The Political Genius of Abraham Lincoln.* New York: Simon & Schuster, 2005.

Kouzes, James M., and Barry Z. Posner. *The Leadership Challenge: How to Make Extraordinary Things Happen in Organizations,* Fifth Edition. New York: Jossey-Bass, 2012.

Kruger, Jeffrey. "Assessing the Creative Spark." Time.com, May 9, 2013, http://business.time.com/2013/05/09/assessing-the-creative-spark/.

Lincoln. Written by Anthony Kushner and directed by Steven Spielberg, 2012.

Margaret. Written by Richard Cottan and directed by James Kent. BBC Films, 2009.

Margaret Thatcher—The Long Walk to Finchley. Produced by Robert Cooper, Kate Triggs, Bethan Jones. BBC Films, 2008.

MacDonald, Alistair. "Former British Prime Minister Margaret Thatcher Dies." *Wall Street Journal,* April 8, 2013.

McMahan, Dana. "Dollywood to Get $300 Million Upgrade." *Today,* August 21, 2013.

Nocera, Joe. "Reading, Math and Grit." *New York Times,* September 7, 2012.

Sampson, Curt. *Hogan.* New York: Broadway Books, 1997.

Seaman, Christopher. "What Is That Conductor Up To?" *Wall Street Journal,* August 3, 2013.

Seeds, Dennis. "Scott Moorehead Uses Culture to Drive Success at The Cellular Connection to the Tune of $600 Million in Sales." *SmartBusiness/ Indianapolis,* November 24, 2013.

Sheridan, Richard. *Joy, Inc.: How We Built a Workplace People Love.* New York: Portfolio/Penguin, 2014.

St. George, Andrew. "Leadership Lessons from the Royal Navy." *McKinsey Quarterly,* January 2013.

————. *Royal Navy Way of Leadership.* London: Cornerstone Publishing, June 2012.

Stein, Joel. "The Real Terminator: How Jerry Brown Scared California Straight." *Bloomberg/Businessweek*, May 5, 2103. http://www.businessweek.com/ articles/2013-04-25/jerry-brown-californias-grownup-governor.

Stone, Brad. "Inside Google's Secret Lab." *Bloomberg Businessweek,* May 22, 2013.

Tebbutt, Judith. *A Long Walk Home.* London: Faber and Faber, 2013.

"Titans of Innovation." Schumpeter, *The Economist,* April 27, 2013.

Vance, Ashlee. "Electric Car Company Chic." *Bloomberg/Businessweek,* July, 28, 2013.

————. "Elon Musk: The 21st Century Industrialist." *Bloomberg/ Businessweek,* September 13, 2012.

"Venetian Glass: Blow Up." *The Economist*, July 6, 2013.

Wikipedia contributors. "Alexander the Great." *Wikipedia, The Free Encyclopedia*. http://en.wikipedia.org/wiki/Alexander_the_Great.

Williams, Thomas, Christopher G. Worley, and Edward E. Lawler. "The Agility Factor." *strategy+business*, April 15, 2013.

"Women Poised to Effectively Lead in Matrix Work Environments, Hay Group Research Finds." Business Wire, May 27, 2012. http://www.businesswire.com/news/home/20120327005180/en#.UxS0-9wrd00.

Index

About the Author

John Baldoni is chair of the leadership development practice of N2growth, a global leadership consultancy. John is an internationally recognized leadership educator, executive coach, and speaks throughout North America and Europe. John is the author of a dozen books, including *Lead with Purpose, Lead Your Boss,* and *The Leader's Pocket Guide.* In 2014 Trust Across America named him to its list of top 100 most trustworthy business experts. Also in 2014 Global Gurus ranked John No. 11 on its list of global leadership experts. John has authored more than 500 leadership columns for a variety of online publications including *Forbes, Harvard Business Review,* and *Bloomberg Businessweek.* His leadership resource website is www.johnbaldoni.com.